DOG BEHAVIOR

Why Dogs Do What They Do

DR. IAN DUNBAR

Frontispiece: Drawing by Betty May Stanbridge, after "Dignity and Impudence," by Sir Edwin Landseer. Drawing pg. 8 also by Betty May Stanbridge, after the Landseer work entitled "A Distinguished Member of the Humane Society." Pg. 7 head study of a spaniel by Sydney Gee Stanbridge, after a Landseer work.

Photo Credits: All photos are by the author, with the exception of: pg. 184 by Colour Library International; pp. 172, 173, 180, 181 by Fritz Prenzel; pp. 73, 76 (above) by Ed Ranson; pg. 177 by Anne Roslin-Williams; pp. 176, 192 and front cover by Vince Serbin; pg. 136 by Louise Van der Meid; pg. 83 by Hank Wesselman. Photos pp. 182, 200 reproduced by gracious permission of Her Majesty Queen Elizabeth II of England.

ISBN 0-87666-671-3

© 1979 by T.F.H. Publications, Inc.

Distributed in the U.S. by T.F.H. Publications, Inc., 211 West Sylvania Avenue, PO Box 427, Neptune, NJ 07753; in England by T.F.H. (Gt. Britain) Ltd., 13 Nutley Lane, Reigate, Surrey; in Canada to the book store and library trade by Beaverbooks Ltd., 150 Lesmill Road, Don Mills, Ontario M38 2T5, Canada; in Canada to the pet trade by Rolf C. Hagen Ltd., 3225 Sartelon Street, Montreal 382, Quebec; in Southeast Asia by Y.W. Ong, 9 Loring 36 Geylang, Singapore 14; in Australia and the South Pacific by Pet Imports Pty. Ltd., P.O. Box 149, Brookvale 2100, N.S.W. Australia. Published by T.F.H. Publications, Inc., Ltd., The British Crown Colony of Hong Kong.

Contents

About the Author

Ian Dunbar Ph.D., B.Sc., B.Vet.Med., M.R.C.V.S.

Ian Dunbar was born in Hertfordshire, England. He attended the University of London, where he read for degrees in physiology and veterinary science. He subsequently obtained a doctorate in animal behavior from the University of California at Berkeley, where he is a member of the Department of Psychology. For the past seven years he has been conducting research into the social and sexual behavior of domestic dogs. Dr. Dunbar lives in California with four goldfish: Silver, Gill, Spot and Rover.

SPANIEL S. Stanbridge.
1906

Acknowledgments

I am surprised that this slender tome has taken me over five years to complete, even though the phases of intensive and purposeful writing have been few and far between, and interspersed with lengthy periods of cerebral gestation. I know that I have bored many friends with *baby stories* of this book: the first step; the first word; the first photograph; and the numerous teething problems etc. I am sincerely grateful to the many people who tolerated, helped and encouraged me during the preparation of this book.

I would particularly like to thank Jill Kuykendall, Mimi Whei-Ping Lou, Michael Buehler, Summer Lee Sankey, Dr. Joseph Anisko, Michael and Alexie Marmot, David Long, Corinne Apostle, Meredith Benz, Dr. and Mrs. Davidson, Hank Wesselman, Barbara Belding, Dr. Charlie Berger, Tom Turner, Jim Baum, Dr. and Mrs. Beach, Dr. James Harris, Dr. Terri McGinnis, Peter and Carol Valk, Daina Bulota, Chuck Young, Jeannine Schulerwill, Michael and Shahiba Strong and many, many others. In addition, special thanks go to Kurt and Jane Wallen, who gave me a copy of *Sirius* and provided a roof over my head during my stay in California.

The initial suggestion to write this book was made by Summer Lee Sankey, aided and abetted by Mrs. Vivian Sutcher, Program Coordinator at the University of California Extension at Berkeley. Some of the material has been published earlier in *Pet News Magazine* and *Our Animals* (a San Francisco SPCA publication) and I would like to express my appreciation to Michael Shapiro and Anne Brice for reinforcing my earlier literary attempts.

The most difficult facet of writing this book has been to achieve a style of presentation that offered an optimal compromise between the stark, stodgy style that is generally intended for an academic audience, and the condescending, wiggly anthropomorphic banter that is often dished out to the dog owning public. I wanted the book to be both informative and enjoyable, but I did not want to *Faust* my soul via worldly advertisement. I am obliged for the editorial assistance of those people who painstakingly read the manuscript and offered criticisms and suggestions that have helped temper a style, that at least I am satisfied with. I am especially indebted to Mimi WheiPing Lou, Professor Frank Beach, Dr. Thelma Rowell, Anne Brice, Michael Buehler, Edoma Ranson and Dr. and Mrs. Davidson.

I am beholden to Kerry Donnelly, formerly of TFH Publications Inc., for putting so much effort into the book's early dogdays at the publishing house. In addition, I would like to thank Beverly Pisano for editing the final manuscript.

Dedication

For St. Agnells

Introduction

In *Sirius,* by Olaf Stapledon, the main character, a Welsh sheep-dog named Sirius, was born with the brain capacity of a human being but with the senses and physique of a dog. Sirius classified human beings in respect of their attitude towards dogs:

There were those who were simply indifferent to dogs, lacking sufficient imagination to enter into any reciprocal relation with them. There were the "dog-lovers," whom he detested. These were folk who sentimentalized dogs, and really had no accurate awareness of them, exaggerating their intelligence and lovableness, mollycoddling them and overfeeding them; and starving their natural impulses of sex, pugnacity and hunting. For this sort, dogs were merely animate and "pathetically human" dolls. Then there were the "dog-detesters," who were either too highbrow to descend to companionship with a dumb animal or too frightened of their own animal nature. Finally, there were the "dog-interested," who combined a fairly accurate sense of the difference between dog and man with a disposition to respect a dog *as a dog,* as a rather remote but essentially like-minded relative.

This book is intended for average everyday dog people, whether they are indifferent toward dogs, whether they love or detest them, or perhaps more important, it is for those who are interested in dogs and wish to better understand how and why domestic dogs behave the way they do.

Despite the fact that dogs and humans have enjoyed a close association for several thousand years, surprisingly, the majority of dog owners are severely lacking in a good understanding of dog behavior. Many owners are relatively unaware of what their dogs are doing, or perhaps more to the point, what they are doing, to

13

their dogs. Pets are persistently subjected to a host of unwarranted anthropomorphisms and much of the time the dog's behavior is misunderstood or misinterpreted. As a result, the relationship between dog and human is rarely given the opportunity to develop fully, and in many cases owning a dog becomes a chore rather than the enjoyment that it should be. This unfortunate situation is frequently exacerbated by inadequate and misguided training procedures on the part of the owner, who all too often provides the majority of social interaction within the domestic environment. However, this state of affairs is not entirely the fault of the owner. Although there are a plethora of books concerning the numerous breed differences of domestic dogs or specialized aspects of training and breeding, there is very little information available to the pet-owning public concerning the general behavior of dogs. Essentially, this book is a review of much of the scientific literature about dog behavior. It is intended primarily for dog owners, but nonetheless, it is hoped that it will also be of some value to trainers, breeders and veterinary surgeons.

In order to understand the behavior and psychology of our best friend, *Canis familiaris,* it is necessary to have a good comprehension of the dog's ancestry, to realize how the behavior of dogs differs from that of wild *Canidae,* and to fully acknowledge the possible ways in which domestication and selective breeding have influenced the behavioral evolution of domestic dogs. Equally as important is the socialization of the puppy within the domestic environment and the development of social and sexual behavior. It is important to appreciate the capabilities and capacities of developing puppies and adult dogs, for these particular physical, sensory and mental constraints are unique to dogs and largely determine the direction and development of their behavioral repertoire. In this respect, emphasis has been afforded to the methods of canine communication. This has immense practical importance for the technique, task, or sometime farce, of conditioning and training procedures, whereby both dog and human endeavor to establish a harmonious and mutually enjoyable domestic synoecy.

1. Puppy Development

One of the most important qualities of a pet dog is its temperament. A dog with a good temperament is a joy to own; an antisocial or fearful dog may be a continual nightmare. In many ways a dog's temperament is largely a result of the processes of *socialization* occurring during puppyhood. This is the most important time of a dog's life, when experiences are new and exert a maximal effect on shaping the dog's future personality and temperament. As such, it is extremely important for the dog owner to fully understand the significance of this crucial stage of development.

Although development is a continual and gradual process, it is sometimes convenient to consider its subdivision into various stages. Nonetheless, it should be realized that this is intended merely as a means of descriptive convenience, since the distinction between progressive stages may be somewhat woolly or arbitrary, to say the least. The following description of developmental stages is not intended as a "Dr. Spot guide to puppy rearing," with a complicated ontogenetic timetable to insure that the puppy is doing all the right things at the right time. Instead, the age at which a puppy enters each period may vary considerably between different breeds. Also, there are usually substantial variations among different litters, and even among individuals within a single litter.

In the interests of brevity, the ages quoted are averages, and for the most part complex breed and individual differences have been ignored. For instance, Scott and Fuller, in their book *Genetics and the Social Behavior of the Dog,* have observed that "by 18 days of age, one-fourth of the Cocker Spaniels were seen wagging their tails, whereas it was not until 30 days of age that Basenjis were observed doing this. At this later age, 83 percent of the Cockers had been seen tail wagging." With the random laws of perversity being what they are, it would be safe to assume that anybody owning a 30 day old Cocker Spaniel would possess one of the 17% of non-tailwaggers, and no doubt, the owner would be unduly concerned about the retarded development of his puppy.

STAGES OF DEVELOPMENT

Puppy development is normally divided into five fairly distinct stages:

PERIOD	AGE OF COMMENCEMENT
1. Neonatal (newborn) period	Birth
2. Transitional period	Eyes open (2 weeks)
3. Socialization period	Ears open (3 weeks)
4. Juvenile period	Weaning (10 weeks)
5. Adult period	Puberty (6 months)

The *neonatal,* or newborn pup is equipped to do little else but suckle and sleep. During the *transitional* period, the pup begins to move about more and more effectively, and first becomes aware of its senses so that by the end of the third week, the littermates begin to establish important social relationships, which are the harbingers of social communication and organization of adult dogs. The bitch gradually becomes less important to the pups and the period of socialization arbitrarily terminates when weaning is completed. The *juvenile* period extends until puberty, whereupon the dog attains sexual maturity and may enter *adult* relationships.

Neonatal Period
The newborn puppy shows little spontaneous movement while still enclosed in the fetal membranes. The bitch normally bites through the membranes and vigorously licks the pup. After taking its first breath, the pup begins squirming from side to side. Initially, there are irregular gasps for air until the fetal fluids have been expelled from the respiratory passages, whereupon the puppy begins to breathe regularly and starts "mewing." It has been suggested that respiration is stimulated by the bitch licking certain areas of the puppy's body, especially the muzzle and the umbilical

The neonatal puppy, such as this one born to a Siberian Husky bitch, is equipped to do little more than suckle and sleep.

area. This is of use when resuscitating fetuses; gentle friction applied to the muzzle and umbilicus will stimulate the puppy's respiratory effort.

The newborn puppy, being blind and deaf, lives in a sensory void. The mother never appears to vocalize to the pup, although the puppy will make vocalizations in response to pain, cold, and hunger. At this early age, the pup's eyelids are closed. However, it may react to very bright lights, especially if the skin pigmentation is sparse and the eyelids are translucent. Newborn puppies are generally deficient in the senses that would be important to an adult dog. Neonatal investigatory behavior depends almost entirely on touch.

The motor capacities are similarly limited. The pup may right itself if turned over onto its back ("righting reflex"), and may crawl slowly, moving its head from side to side ("rooting reflex"). The puppy does not move towards specific stimuli, but instead wanders around aimlessly and it is purely trial and error whether or not it establishes contact with the bitch and other pups. However, at this stage it is normal for the bitch to compensate for

The cautious bitch, always concerned about her newborn puppies, will retrieve any one that wanders too far from the nesting box.

this deficiency, and she will usually retrieve any pup which gets too far away. Generally, a puppy will attempt to suckle when it encounters anything warm and soft, whether it be a teat, another pup's tail, paw, or ear ("sucking reflex"). When it locates a teat, it will suck vigorously, pumping the mammary gland with its forepaws and pushing hard with its hind legs. Unlike kittens, pups do not have a *specific* teat preference. Nonetheless, given the choice they will tend to suckle from the more pendulous inguinal teats. The tendency to suckle is very strong. (If a pup is unable to suckle, it won't live past one or two days). In an experiment where puppies were bottle fed, on average, they suckled for eighty minutes a day. If however, they were fed from bottles with very large holes, so that their food requirement was satisfied by only thirteen minutes of feeding a day, the pups would show post-feeding displacement sucking, even during sleep.

18

After feeding, when puppies come into contact with other litter-mates, they will settle down in a heap and usually fall asleep in a communal pile. This is probably a method of heat conservation, since until three or four weeks of age, the ability of a pup to regulate its own body temperature has not fully matured. The pups will group together in a heap if it is too cold and spread out and sleep singly should it get too warm.

During the first two weeks of life, puppies spend approximately ninety percent of their time asleep, and awake only to feed or be cleaned by the dam. At this stage, the bitch will spend the majority of time with her pups, leaving the litter box only to eat or relieve herself. Periodically, the bitch will poke the puppies with her nose, which immediately initiates rooting activity. At this stage,

After littermates have eaten, they will come together as a group and settle down in a heap, to fall asleep in a communal pile. This is probably a method of heat conservation, since the pup who is not yet three to four weeks old has not developed the ability to regulate its own body temperature. Should it get too warm for the pups they will spread out and sleep singly.

the pups do not have voluntary control over their eliminatory functions. These functions are reflex actions and are in most cases initiated by the bitch. The mother will lick the pups' anal and genital area, which causes reflex urination and defecation. The bitch often eats the feces in order to keep the nest clean. As the pups grow older, they sleep less, and their feeding periods are more prolonged.

Very young puppies have a mask-like appearance and display no facial expressions; they don't even wag their tails. The puppies grow in size and strength, but essentially their behavior remains the same. The modest behavioral repertoire of the helpless pups is supplemented by maternal behavior of the bitch, who offers warmth and comfort and provides sustenance. Maternal actions also stimulate elimination.

Transitional Period

The transitional stage is a period of very rapid maturation of the senses, and of major changes in motor behavior patterns. The first major change occurs when the eyes open at about thirteen days. The ears open toward the end of the third week, whereupon the investigatory behavior is now based primarily on sight and sound. By this time, the puppy has developed the ability to crawl backwards as well as forwards, but more likely it will attempt to walk rather than crawl. When as young as two weeks, the pup may begin to clumsily lap milk from a saucer, and within a week, most will have acquired the ability to stand and drink fairly efficiently. The mother may regurgitate partially digested, warm, semi-solid food to supplement the pup's liquid diet.

Strong approach behavior begins to develop and the puppy will often engage in playful biting and pawing. The puppy will attempt to bite and chew, but this is largely ineffective because the milk teeth have only just started to come through. The upper canine teeth emerge at the end of the third week. Throughout this week, there is considerable improvement in the ability to learn. It is possible to train puppies to perform a response for food reward as early as fifteen days of age. Similarly, three week old puppies soon develop the ability to make an association between a painful experience and the appropriate avoidance behavior.

In the early weeks of a pup's life, investigatory behavior is based on sight and sound. As he matures, the pup will become naturally curious about his surroundings and will investigate them in other ways, such as by smell.

Socialization Period

At this age, pups still spend the majority of the day asleep. In the newborn puppy, there are few brain waves. There is virtually no difference between the EEG (electroencephalogram) of a puppy when sleeping or awake until three weeks, when there is a stage of rapid brain development, evidenced by a sudden increase in amplitude of brain waves during the wakeful state. This change is presumably associated with the opening of the eyes and development of the visual cortex. The retina fully matures at approximately four weeks of age and the puppy is soon capable of discerning form. By eight weeks, the puppy has acquired complete visual capacity, at which time the EEG is essentially similar to that of an adult. During the first few weeks of the socialization period, most sensory and motor functions undergo notable maturation. However, brain development is far from complete, since the myelinization of association areas of the cortex is an extremely protracted process. This may bear some relation to the gradual improvement in learning abilities that occur throughout the juvenile period.

In conjunction with the maturation of perceptual abilities, during the socialization period, the pups rapidly acquire and exercise new skills in walking, running and manipulating objects. The pups are now capable of a wide variety of facial expressions,

"Mimi," left, and "Chevron," right, sister and brother from the same litter at six weeks of age.

notably those involving ear and lip movements. Similarly, they now practice a broad selection of vocalizations and communicative body postures and movements which represent component foundations of the broad repertoire of adult social and sexual behavior patterns. Puppies usually start to bark at approximately three weeks of age, and tail wagging develops on the average during the third or fourth week. There are striking breed differences in the time of onset. As mentioned earlier, most Cocker Spaniels will begin to wag their tails around two and a half weeks, whereas with Basenjis this will not occur until about four weeks. This is probably related to a variation of the required *wag-threshold of stimulation* rather than a differential rate of development between the two breeds; Cockers will wag their tails at the slightest provocation, whereas a Basenji will require a much stronger stimulus. Tail wagging probably represents an expression of pleasurable emotion during social encounters and is most apparent during friendly or submissive situations. It has been suggested that it serves a social function much like the human smile.

From an early age, puppies adopt a certain pattern of excretory behavior and are unlikely to soil their nest. Sometime after three weeks, when the locomotor activity is sufficiently developed, the pups will attempt to leave the sleeping area in order to urinate immediately after waking. At first, they will not go very far, but soon they will establish specific spots to relieve themselves and begin to perform cursory investigations beforehand. Afterwards they will feed, and then they are cleaned by the bitch before indulging in a period of play. After a short while, the puppies will again defecate and perhaps urinate as well. This convenient sequence of events considerably facilitates house-training, since the owner has almost as much of a forewarning as the puppy. The puppy may be put outside immediately after waking. After feeding time, the owner may play with the pup and carefully watch for signs that the animal is about to relieve itself once more, whereupon the potential eliminator can be immediately transported to a suitable area.

The period of socialization is the time when the puppy becomes capable of forming social relationships with other dogs, notably the dam and littermates. As the pups get older, interactions with the mother become more infrequent and the associations within the litter assume prime importance. The mother begins to leave the pups for longer periods, and the protracted process of weaning may start as early as five weeks. Some mothers will have ceased milk production by seven weeks, but more usually, final weaning is not complete until at least ten weeks.

Puppies start to follow each other almost as soon as they can walk, especially if the leading puppy is carrying something such as a toy or piece of food. By five weeks of age, the litter often runs around together in a little pack. Puppies spend a large portion of their time involved in playful interactions. They will climb over their littermates, clumsily pawing and mouthing each other. They will lick faces and attempt to chew ears and bite elusive tails. They will start pouncing on each other, grabbing other puppies by the scruff and growling as they shake their heads from side to side. As they grow older, the longer and sharper teeth often locate a sensitive spot, which elicits a distressful yelp of pain. At this very early age, the pup begins to learn exactly how hard it may bite or be bitten before pain is felt. The young dog learns to inhibit biting at a stage before the jaws are sufficiently developed to do much harm.

When about seven weeks old, the pups will begin group attacks on littermates. Although the choice of victim is usually temporary, quite often a smaller or weaker individual is constantly picked on. Two puppies will hold the ears, scruff, or tail of a victim, and the rest will playfully attack the middle. Occasionally, these playful attacks may prove too injurious, particularly in some of the more aggressive breeds. Even if the victim is removed to avoid serious injury, the pups will simply attack another. In these situations, the only solution is to isolate the pups into groups of three. Even if victimization still occurs, one pup may hold the front end and another the rear but there will be no one to attack the middle.

The large amount of time that is spent playing is of utmost importance in the physical and behavioral maturation of the dog. During this time, perceptual and locomotor skills are developed with continual practice and exercise. These are skills which will be required for hunting and fighting and would be essential for survival in the wild. It is likely that the social relationships that the pups establish with littermates are the building blocks of social organization in adulthood. The emphasis on play-fighting offers an opportunity to learn the relevant social signals that are necessary to control aggression among adult animals. It is im-

Puppies learn to inhibit the strength of their bites at a stage before the jaws are sufficiently developed to cause much damage.

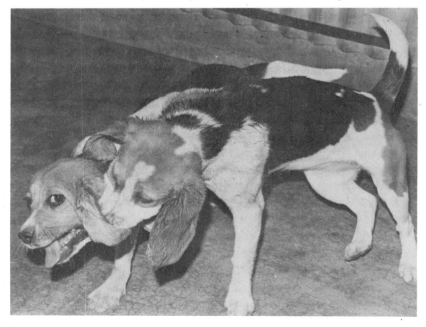

Puppies greatly love to play and romp. This Beagle litter seems to be finding some fun at the feet of a human companion.

perative that the developing puppies are thoroughly familiar with these canine social pleasantries before they embark on social relationships with other dogs. A harmless puppy may be afforded a certain amount of playful license from an adult dog, but this adult will only rarely tolerate impudence or disrespect from a bumptious juvenile.

Some fragments of play behavior may be interpreted as an early manifestation of sexual behavior. Puppies as young as four or five weeks may exhibit mounting and pelvic thrusting behavior, although at this age the sex organs are not fully developed.

The behavioral development of a young puppy is constrained by the maturation of its anatomical and perceptual abilities. That is, it cannot run until it can walk, it cannot walk until it can stand, and it cannot stand until it has adequate strength and muscular coordination. Similarly, it cannot hear or see properly until its ears and eyes have opened, and it cannot learn until its brain is sufficiently developed.

By the time it is seven weeks old, a puppy is capable of performing many components of adult behavior. However, puppies often express a succession of different fragments of adult behavior patterns, that are hopelessly intermingled and inappropriate to the particular social context. A puppy may go through a series of prey-killing manuevers and attack another puppy, or pounce on the bitch's tail, only to exhibit mounting and thrusting behavior as a finalé. With experience and continued practice, the puppy steadily learns to discriminate between the multitude of social signals and their appropriate social response.

Juvenile Period

During the juvenile period, the behavior patterns do not change as such. There is a gradual improvement of motor skills as the puppy grows in strength and activity. At the same time, the puppies continue to learn the relevance of their behaviors and they begin to exhibit the correct behavior in the right place, at the right time.

Until they are about twelve weeks old, puppies will be content to stay within range of their mother, and snooze for a good part of each day. At twelve weeks, the pups will begin to explore outer surroundings.

The juvenile puppy shows an increased tendency to explore his environment. In an experiment where puppies were raised in a one acre field, the pups remained within twenty feet of the nest box and did not start to explore the remainder of the field until they were approximately twelve weeks old. In the wild, wolf cubs remain fairly close to the den and only investigate the surrounding area. The mother and other members of the pack will continue to regurgitate food for the young. A young juvenile is still unable to hunt for itself, even though it has been weaned. Puppies become capable of hunting at about the time the second teeth begin to appear, around four months of age. The permanent teeth are all present by six months, at which time the growth curve has almost flattened out and the puppy is about two-thirds of its adult size.

The learning capacities are fully developed at the beginning of the juvenile period. In fact, thereafter, it becomes increasingly more difficult and time-consuming to train a dog, probably because new learning is often dissonant with established behavior patterns. This is all the more reason to start the training program as early as possible, even though it may be limited by the puppies' short attention span and poor motor coordination.

For male dogs, one of the first signs of the onset of puberty is when the male assumes the characteristic leg-lifting urination posture. In 1942, the Nobel prize winner, Niko Tinbergen, studied the territorial behavior of Eskimo dogs in East Greenland, which is colorfully described in his book *Curious Naturalists*. The dogs lived in packs of five or ten. Immature males did not defend the pack territory and they would roam over neighborhood territories. Once the dogs reached sexual maturity, they began to observe territorial boundaries. With two dogs, the first copulation, the first defense of territory and the first avoidance of strange territory all occurred within one week.

The time course of puberty is different for male and female dogs. In the bitch, puberty represents the dividing line between being a juvenile and being an adult. One day the female will show no signs of sexual attractiveness or receptiveness and she has little interest in male dogs, whereas the next day she may be in heat. Her vulva will become swollen and show signs of a bloody discharge. Male dogs find her extremely attractive and similarly, she will begin to display an increasing interest in her male suitors.

Within a few days she will become receptive and allow mating for the first time.

In the male dog, however, puberty is a protracted transitional phase between the juvenile and adult periods. At four months of age, male pups may begin to show an avid interest in adult females that are in heat. At this age, juvenile males will readily mount a female, although normally they do not acquire the ability to achieve an intromission and execute a fertile mating until seven or eight months of age. Similarly, they may start to lift their leg when urinating at four or five months, but it may be several months before this posture is employed exclusively. A year old, sexually mature, male dog still has a lot to learn before it becomes socially mature.

Adult Period

The development of sexual maturity marks the onset of the adult period; the dog is capable of mating and the bitch comes into heat for the first time.

Dogs increase in size and strength during their second year and throughout adulthood they continue to acquire a wealth of information about their environment, right up to their sunset years. Old age may begin as early as seven years in some of the larger breeds, such as the Great Dane, but as late as twelve years in most toy breeds.

SOCIALIZATION

For a long time, it has been recognized that it is extremely difficult to tame an adult wild animal. There are very few examples of adult timber wolves that have been successfully socialized with humans. It is similarly difficult to socialize an adult dog that has had limited contact with humans during its formative months. It is easier to train young dogs than to try to teach an old dog new tricks. Intensive research on this subject has been done by Clarence Pfaffenberger when training guide dogs for the blind. It was proposed that delayed socialization with humans interfered with the suitability of dogs that were to be trained for specialized tasks. It was suggested that during the early development of a puppy there is a period when social contacts exert a maximal effect on

In order for a pup such as this Beagle to be sufficiently socialized with humans and other dogs, he should be removed from the litter at between six and eight weeks. Such socialization is especially important to a pup who was purchased in a pet shop, where he probably received less attention that he requires.

social development. This phase was termed the "critical period of socialization," and is thought to be the optimal stage for the establishment of primary social relationships with fellow dogs, humans, or other species. John Paul Scott and John Fuller, in their book *Genetics and Social Behavior of the Dog*, described the critical period as "A special time in life when a small amount of experience will produce a great effect on later behavior." In many ways this is similar to a phenomenon that Konrad Lorenz observed in precocious birds. He demonstrated that newly-hatched geese formed social relationships within the first few hours of hatching, and he termed this process *pragung*, which has been translated as "imprinting."

At the beginning of the socialization period, puppies show strong approach behavior to anything new in the environment. Characteristically, they will persistently investigate novel stimuli and confidently approach and follow virtually anything that moves. However, by the time the pups are five weeks old, there is an increasing tendency to avoid novel objects and unfamiliar situations, which eventually overshadows the initially strong approach behavior.*

It appears that the optimal time for a puppy to develop social attachments toward its own or another species is approximately between three and thirteen weeks of age.

The "critical period" commences fairly abruptly when both the eyes and ears open by about three weeks of age. At this time, the pup is literally bombarded with new and intriguing stimuli, which exert a maximal effect on shaping the dog's future personality and temperament. However, the termination of this critical period is less precise, and in reality it probably never ends. Most certainly the dog requires continual contact and interaction with others as its social development progresses into adulthood. In view of this elastic time limit, perhaps it is better to consider the socialization phase as a "sensitive period." With the exception that within the first two or three weeks of life the puppy is blind, deaf, and cannot smell too well and consequently is not fully aware of the environment, to some extent the ease of socialization is inversely proportional to age.

In the wild, this phenomenon has several adaptive implications. During the period when cubs show strong approach behavior, they normally remain close to the den and are only likely to encounter the dam, littermates, and perhaps other members of the pack. In this way they will invariably become socialized with members of their own species. When the cubs become older, they will readily continue to approach animals that they know, thus reinforcing the primary social relationships that have already been established. On the other hand, they will become extremely wary of other species, as the tendency to avoid novel stimuli increases.

---

*An experiment was performed where puppies were raised in a field with limited contact for the first three months of life. At the ages of three, seven, and fourteen weeks the puppies were placed in a room with a human observer, ten minutes a day for a week. When they were three weeks of age, the puppies approached the observer almost immediately, but when seven weeks old the pups took two days before they made a single social approach. The fourteen week old puppies were wild and unapproachable and never came close to the observer.

In the domestic environment, puppies may similarly become socialized towards their human companions when the litter is raised with plentiful human contact. It is therefore extremely important that the pups are taken away from the litter at the optimal time. If, as an adult, the dog will be expected to amiably socialize with other dogs and humans, during the impressionable and sensitive critical period the puppy should be exposed to a variety of such. This may sound obvious, but all too often the obvious is neglected. Some puppies are removed from their mother and littermates as early as three or four weeks, and subsequently raised in apartments with very little contact with other dogs. It is hardly surprising that often these dogs will be asocial or antisocial toward members of their own species, since they have had little opportunity to learn and practice the social conduct that is essential in the canine world. In some cases, they may even refuse to mate with other dogs. Alternatively, they sometimes redirect their sexual advances toward their owners, or perhaps attempt to mount the cat or legs of embarrassed visitors. However, if pups have been raised in a pet shop or kennel environment until about ten weeks of age, it is improbable that they will have been overcome with an abundance of human attention during the sensitive period, and

Your pup should ideally be sufficiently socialized towards humans, or else the amount of time and energy required to train him will be considerable.

The bitch will share her food with the pups but will also allow them to suckle.

they may not become adequately socialized towards humans. Instead, they may grow to be wary of people. Such dogs will be difficult to train and will most likely make unsuitable pets or companions.

In order to achieve sufficient socialization with dogs and humans, the best time to take the pup from the litter would be between six and eight weeks. At this stage, the pup has received about four weeks socialization with other dogs before introduction to the world of people. This is of special importance if the pup is bought from a pet shop or commercial puppy farm, where it would be unlikely to receive the amount of attention that a conscientious breeder or individual dog owner might give it. If for some reason, it is impossible to bring the dog home until it is two and a half or three months old, the prospective owner should ensure that the puppy receives enough contact with a variety of humans. It should go without saying that during this period, human contact should be kind and non-threatening. Similarly, if the pup must be removed from the dam and litter early, let it meet other dogs at home.*

* Of course, the owner should make sure that canine visitors have been recently vaccinated against distemper, hepatitis, leptospirosis, and rabies. Until the puppy has been fully immunized, it should not be allowed out on the streets, where it might encounter other dogs that might be carriers of such diseases.

Michael Fox has suggested that within the critical period there is a further sensitive period at about eight weeks of age, at which time the pup is particularly sensitive to psychological trauma. In an experiment, he gave five, eight and twelve week old domestic puppies a mild electric shock when they approached humans. They were rested for a week and then re-tested. Five week old dogs continued to approach the experimenter; perhaps they were too young for permanent retention of the aversive conditioning and quickly forgot the traumatic experience. Similarly, the three month old pups never exhibited avoidance behavior; in fact, they ran faster when being shocked. It was postulated that they were strongly socialized with humans, and that they would attempt to reduce anxiety by running toward the experimenter. However, the eight week old puppies showed almost permanent conditioning of the avoidance response and were extremely wary of approaching the experimenter.

Quite often this additional sensitive period coincides with the time that the puppy is taken away from its mother and littermates. The pup should receive plenty of attention from its human companions, especially during the first couple of weeks in its new home. An effort should be made to allow the pup to quickly familiarize itself with the daily routine, so that it may feel secure in its new surroundings.

An effort should be made to allow the pup to familiarize itself with the daily routine, so that it may feel secure in its new surroundings. However, on occasions, situations that provoke mild anxiety may increase the ease with which puppies may be socialized towards humans. Scheduled short term deprivation, such as leaving the puppy alone overnight, increases the dependency of the dog on the owner, particularly if reinforced with attention and feeding in the morning.

It is far better to try and get the dog started on the right foot (or paw). A dog that has not had the benefit of a good environment as a puppy need not be considered a lost cause. But, if a dog has not been adequately socialized towards humans, the amount of time and energy required for training will be considerable, and probably well beyond the patience of most dog owners. Remember, prevention is better (and much easier) than cure.

These lovable Beagle puppies are wagging their tails because, quite obviously, they enjoy a very friendly relationship with the author!

2. Why Does A Dog Wag Its Tail?

Why does a dog behave like a dog? Why not like a cat or a human being? The answer is really quite straightforward and has been simply expressed by T.S. Eliot in his poem "The Ad-Dressing of Cats:"

> So first your memory I'll jog,
> And say a cat is not a dog.

This may seem oversimplistic, but as we have seen in the developing puppy, to a large extent its behavior is very much limited by the maturation of sensory and motor skills. The same principle applies to adult dogs. Adult behavior does not only develop throughout puppyhood. It is the result of numerous years of evolution, during which dog behavior has become specialized toward life and survival in the wild. Thus, in an adult dog the behavior is very much specialized, or limited by, the evolution and development of: the dog's anatomy; the dog's sensory impression of the environment; and the dog's brain, especially those areas which coordinate sensory input and motor activities. It is important to realize and understand these limitations because they are very different from equivalent constraints on human behavior.

Canine Capacities and Capabilities

Many behaviors are severely restricted by a dog's anatomy, and it would be true to say that a dog behaves like a dog largely because it has a dog's body. Thus, it will not manipulate objects the way a human can, climb trees like a cat, fly like a bird or swim like a fish because it does not have the specialized anatomical structures to do so. Instead, it will run, bury bones, and wag its tail like a dog.

One of the reasons many people have difficulty in understanding dog behavior is that they tend to see things from a human point of view. Humans see, hear, smell and experience their environment with human senses, and they respond to these stimuli with human brains and bodies. The dog, on the other hand, sees life differently. It experiences life from a dog's point of view. A dog can hear sounds that humans are unable to and it can experience smells that are well beyond the capabilities of the human nose. A dog can see things that humans cannot see, just as humans can see things that dogs cannot. Dogs and humans may be exposed to the same physical environment and yet perceive it differently. Obviously, this will have a marked effect on behavior.

The parts of the brain that are devoted to processing sensory information, particularly from the senses of smell and hearing, are much better developed in dogs than in humans. Generally, the dog is aware of more sophisticated sensory information about its surroundings. The human brain, however, has a much larger cerebral cortex and far superior powers of reasoning. What humans lack in the way of sensory information about their environment, they adequately make up for by deductive reasoning.

DOGS' BODIES

Although there are a variety of shapes and sizes of dogs, the general anatomy remains the same for all breeds. The dog's body is a product of years of evolution, during which it has become ideally suited to perform specialized behaviors that were best adapted for survival. These specializations are now reflected in the natural way of life for dogs, both domestic and wild.

Limbs

Dogs' limbs have been specialized for endurance running at high speeds. The fastest mammal is the cheetah, which can reach speeds of up to 70 mph over short distances. Some breeds of dog can reach 40 mph , and the wolf about 30 mph. However, canines have greater endurance and can maintain their speed over longer distances.

Dogs are *digitigrade*; that is, they stand on their toes, unlike bears, for example, which are *plantigrade*, and walk on the soles of

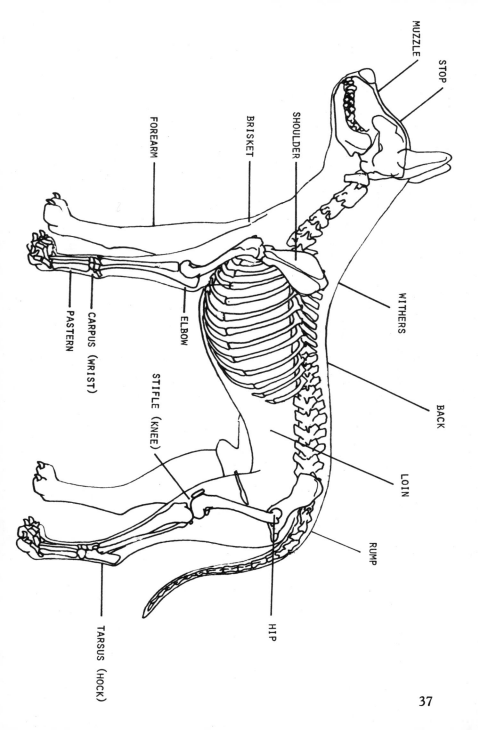

MUZZLE

STOP

FOREARM

BRISKET

SHOULDER

WITHERS

BACK

PASTERN

CARPUS (WRIST)

ELBOW

STIFLE (KNEE)

LOIN

RUMP

TARSUS (HOCK)

HIP

37

Above:
Recently-weaned puppies already have attained the ability to chew hard, kibbled food.

Opposite:
Dogs know how to effectively use their paws and jaws for eating. The nonretractable claws of a dog such as this Alaskan Malamute help him to hold a bone.

their feet. As a result, dogs are able to run faster than bears, but a dog would find it more difficult to maintain balance while standing on its hind feet. The same principle applies to humans. Short distance runners tend to sprint on their toes, as compared to the slower and much more cumbersome "executive joggers."

The dog is limited in the amount of abduction of its front limbs. The front leg may only be moved away from the body a few degrees, since the skin that covers the chest wall also encloses the upper two thirds of the humerus. This holds the limb against the chest wall and limits the movement of the shoulder joint to a backward and forward motion as employed in walking and running. In this respect, the horse is even more specialized, since the skin covering the chest almost totally encloses the elbow joint. In humans however, the arms may be abducted throughout a complete semi-circle and may be rotated in all directions. Thus, because of the dog's specialization for long distance running ability, they have lost a great deal of movement in their front legs.

Paws

A dog does not have the manual dexterity of a human and there are several reasons for this. Humans are bipedal, and as such, their hands are free to manipulate and carry objects. A dog has evolved to stand and run on all four legs, and when it raises its front legs from the ground it could easily fall over. Some dogs have become quite adept at sitting on their haunches and begging, and some can even walk short distances on their hind legs. Even so, a dog would have great difficulty in holding a fountain pen or a cup of tea as we humans do. Human hands have more digits and longer fingers with a thumb in apposition, greatly facilitating the manipulation of objects.

Dogs have only four toes on each of their front and hind feet. The dog has a vestigial toe (or dewclaw) on each leg, a vestigial "thumb" on the foreleg and a vestigial "big toe" on the hind. (Some breeds, such as a Great Pyrenees, have two dewclaws). These serve no particular function and are usually removed at an early age to prevent the possibility of injury. This reduction in the number of digits is a further specialization for running. Many ungulates, such as the cow, have two digits, and the horse has only one.

Compared to a dog, a cat has a greater ability for manipulating objects because of its sharp retractile claws, which it keeps sharpened for hunting, fighting and climbing trees, whereas a dog will use its jaws for hunting and fighting. A dog has nonretractable claws, which are comparatively blunt and are used mainly for traction when moving over rough terrain. Dogs may use their claws to some extent for holding objects, but are generally more clumsy.

Another specialization for locomotion is that all dogs have partially webbed feet, which probably evolved as a specialization for walking on soft sand or snow. In most dogs, the skin between the toes extends to the second phalanges, whereas the Newfoundland is unique in that the skin extends to the end of the third. The

Dogs may use their paws to some extent for manipulating objects. This Alaskan Malamute uses her jaws quite effectively while eating a bone.

degree of webbing is similarly prominent in other breeds that have been selectively bred for working in water, such as the Otterhound. Although dogs are far from being expert swimmers, *Field and Stream* has reported that dog swimming races were held in the 1800's.

Jaws

A dog's lips are not as mobile as those of other animals, such as llamas and chimpanzees, but their dentition has become extremely specialized. Not only are a dog's teeth efficient tools for eating flesh and bones; they are also formidable weapons. The long canine teeth are used for making deep bites when catching hold of prey, and occasionally may inflict serious wounds during aggressive encounters. Often, the wounds are complicated as the dog pulls its head away, causing deep tears in the skin or flesh. The specialized carnassial flesh-eating teeth work like a pair of self-sharpening scissors when used for shearing flesh; other molars are for crushing bones. The incisors are used primarily for nibbling, either at food, fleas, etc.

Dogs and Eagles

Unlike eagles, dogs cannot fly, because they do not have wings. However, once on the ground, eagles cannot run as fast as a dog can. Hopefully, this absurdly obvious example adequately illustrates the essence of this section. Specialization of limbs for a particular function usually limits their usefulness for other purposes. Thus, a bird will use its wings almost exclusively for flight, whereas human arms and hands are specialized for manipulating objects. Although dogs cannot fly and are less dextrous than humans, they can otherwise run faster and for longer distances than birds or humans can. This represents an evolutionary behavioral "trade-off." In other words, "what one gains on the roundabouts one loses on the swings."

SENSE AND NONSENSE

Although dogs may not be as dextrous as humans, in many ways their senses are far superior. In fact, the senses of smell and hearing are so superior that dogs entertain a considerably different sensory world compared to their human companions. A dog hears sounds that are inaudible to human ears, smells odors which humans would never dream possible of sniffing, sees things which humans are unable to see. To acknowledge these elementary dog-human differences is half the way to understanding a *dog as a dog*. However, the constant failure of humans to appreciate these distinctions is one of the greatest confoundings when attempting to understand dog behavior. Not only do humans perceive their surroundings with human senses, but they often adopt the habit of assuming that dogs should do likewise. This myopic point of view is, of course, *nonsense*.

Vision

Dogs are virtually color-blind and although their binocular vision is inferior to man's, they see exceedingly well at night. Generally, a dog does not attend so much to details or texture, but instead recognizes objects by their general form and is extremely sensitive to movement. It should be remembered that most *Canidae* are crepuscular (active in twilight). Thus, night vision is a great advantage. The reasons underlying dogs' superior night vision are twofold. In the retina there are two types of cells that are sensitive to light, rods and cones. Rods are very sensitive to low intensities of light, whereas cones are primarily for color vision. Dogs' retinas have a significantly higher rod/cone ratio than the human retina, so that the dog is better adapted for seeing in dim light, and humans have superior color vision. Although color vision in the dog is virtually non-existent, they are capable of discriminating some colors by different intensities.

Light rays enter the eye via the pupil, and then pass through the lens and retina to be absorbed by the choroid layer, which is extremely rich in blood vessels. This is the reason why the pupil appears to be red in photographs taken with an electronic flash. However, at the back of the dogs' choroid is a reflective surface called the tapetum. While a dog's eyes are becoming adapted to seeing in dim light, finger-like projections of the tapetum move forward and line the inner surface of the choroid to form a reflective layer behind the retina. Consequently, once the light has passed through the retina in the dark-adapted eye, instead of being absorbed by the choroid, it is reflected straight back through the retina by the tapetum. Thus, the light rays pass through the retina

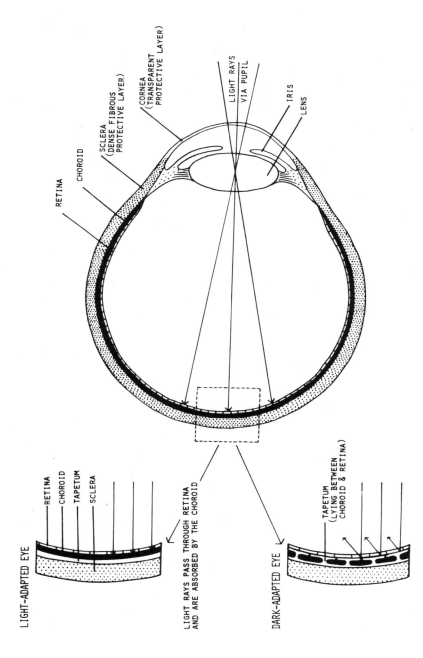

RETINA

CHOROID

SCLERA
(DENSE FIBROUS
PROTECTIVE LAYER)

CORNEA
(TRANSPARENT
PROTECTIVE LAYER)

LIGHT RAYS
VIA PUPIL

IRIS

LENS

LIGHT-ADAPTED EYE

RETINA
CHOROID
TAPETUM
SCLERA

LIGHT RAYS PASS THROUGH RETINA
AND ARE ABSORBED BY THE CHOROID

DARK-ADAPTED EYE

TAPETUM
(LYING BETWEEN
CHOROID & RETINA)

LIGHT RAYS PASS THROUGH RETINA
AND ARE REFLECTED BY THE TAPETUM

44

twice and have a greater chance of activating the light sensitive rods. In the dog, the tapetum is usually green or yellowish-green, and this is the color that dark-adapted dogs' eyes appear in car headlamps.

Birds and ungulates have eyes at the sides of their heads, enabling them to see in all directions. In the dog, the eyes are located toward the front and they are unable to see behind him. Nevertheless, in some breeds (such as the Greyhound) the total field of vision approaches 270 degrees, which is about 70 degrees greater than that in humans. However, the field of binocular vision is about half that of humans. In those breeds with long pointed noses, such as the Borzoi, Saluki and Greyhound, the angle of binocular vision is about 70 degrees, whereas it approximates 80 degrees in breeds with short muzzles, such as the King Charles Spaniel, Pekingese and Bulldog. In humans, the field of binocular vision is about 140 degrees. Thus, compared to humans, dogs are better at detecting peripheral movements, yet inferior in the perception of distance.

Hearing

A dog's sense of hearing is highly developed. Sounds that a human can hear at a hundred yards a dog can hear over a quarter of a mile away. Moreover, dogs are capable of hearing ultrasonic sounds. In humans, the maximum audible frequency is approximately 20,000 cycles per second, whereas it has been demonstrated that a dog can perceive at least 35,000 cps. A rat can perceive 40,000 cps , a cat 50,000 and a bat approximately 70,000 cycles per second. Some reports have even suggested that a dog can hear sounds with a frequency of between 70,000 and a hundred thousand cycles per second. Ultrasonic hearing is the principle behind the high frequency 'silent' dog whistle. Although the high frequencies are inaudible to humans, they may easily be heard by dogs. This capacity is of importance when dogs are hunting. Many animals, such as rodents, often communicate with high frequency sounds, which help the dog locate a potential meal.

A dog's ears have a further advantage over human ears. The mobile ear pinnas are ideally constructed for the precise location of sound. The ear pinnas may be pointed in separate directions, or they may be both directed forward at the same time. Human ears, on either side of the head, determine only vague sound directions. Experiments have shown that a dog could easily locate the direction of sound when placed in the center of a six yard diameter circle of sixty electric buzzers that were placed approximately one foot apart. In a similar experiment, buzzers were placed behind two planks that were less than eight inches apart. It was found that the dog could discriminate the source of the sound from a distance of up to five yards.

Smell

Herein lies the great difference. The dog's nose is its natural forté, a canine *pièce de resistance*. Some humans have developed a keen sense of smell, for instance those involved in wine tasting or the manufacture of perfumes. Nonetheless, the area of the brain that is concerned with smell, the rhinecephalon, is considerably more developed in dogs than in humans. In the dog it has been estimated that there are some 200 million olfactory cells compared with about five million in humans. However, the canine sense of smell is much more than forty times better than that of humans. Not only are the number of olfactory cells important; so is their sensitivity. A variety of examples explain the incredible capacity of the dog's sense of smell. One of the odors of perspiration is butyric acid, and one gram of it contains seven sextillion molecules, which by any standards is an extremely large number of molecules. If this gram of butyric acid was diluted in the air of a ten story office building, a human would only be able to identify the smell of perspiration upon entering the building. However, a dog could detect butyric acid if the same amount had evaporated into the air up to three hundred feet above a city the size of Philadelphia. Similarly, a solution of salt is said to be odorless to humans, but dogs have been reported to smell as little as one teaspoonful of salt in thirteen gallons of water. It has been suggested that olfaction in the dog is up to one million times superior to man. Much like the difference between the moon and a moribund wren's egg.

Dogs' incredible sense of smell has been employed in several ways. Several breeds of trail hounds and hunting dogs are used for tracking and flushing out game and truffles. Bloodhounds are renowned for their tracking ability, and similarly, St. Bernards

46

An animal's sense of smell is very important, especially when investigating a newcomer.

have been successful in locating people buried deep in snow. In Holland and Denmark dogs have been used to locate gas leaks. In many cases dogs have proven to be more reliable than scientific instruments. Dogs have been used by customs agents and police to detect contraband, such as coffee, tobacco and opium. Dogs may locate such substances even if they have been wrapped in twenty seven layers of polythene paper. Recently, dogs have begun being trained to sniff out explosives in cargo or aboard aircrafts, because modern technology has failed to devise an effective mechanical "sniffer" that can compete with the nose of a trained mutt.

It has been shown that following a few days of fasting, a dog's sense of smell may increase threefold, whereas if a dog eats as little as one gram of fatty acid its powers of olfaction are greatly reduced. This makes sense, since following a feast the dog has no immediate need for an acute sense of smell to track down prey, whereas this may be of the utmost importance to a hungry dog. This is one reason why owners have adopted the habit of fasting their hounds or gun dogs prior to taking them hunting.

An experienced dog has only to run along a fresh animal track for as little as twenty yards before it can determine in which direction the animal was going.

A good portion of the evidence attesting to dogs' unique sense of smell is in the form of anecdotal observations. The British naturalist Romanes performed several experiments with his setter. In one, he set off at the head of a line of 12 men, all wearing new Wellington boots. Each man trod in the footsteps of the preceding person. After several hundred yards, Romanes and five others turned at right angles, with the other six turning in the opposite direction. When the setter was released, it easily followed the trail and found its master. In another experiment, six people threw handkerchiefs in the presence of a dog, which was then allowed to sniff the fingers of one person and then reliably retrieve the handkerchief to the appropriate owner. In this situation, the dog was not infallible when distinguishing between identical twins. However, in a second experiment using young German Shepherd Dogs that belonged to the British Police Force, two identical twins walked along together and after a certain distance they split up and went in different directions; one of the twins dropped a handkerchief at the point of divergence. In this situation the dog had little difficulty in locating the correct twin, presumably because at the point of separation the dog had two scents for comparison, whereas in the first experiment it would retrieve the first handkerchief it found with an odor that closely resembled the fingers that it had smelled. Thus, it would always retrieve the handkerchief of one of the twins but would not always choose the correct twin.

In the summer of 1934, Leon Whitney, a noted dog authority, used his Bloodhounds to find a lost baby. The dogs held their muzzles in the air and started upwind without putting their noses to the ground. They ran 3/8ths of a mile through a crowd of about two hundred people, to a house in which the little girl was found. Bloodhounds have been known to follow trails that were several days old, and one Bloodhound, named Nick Carter, successfully ran a trail that was 105 hours old.

Taste and Touch

Little is known about dogs' sense of taste. In general, dogs aren't finnicky feeders, as they will usually eat anything that remotely resembles food. In fact, a dog rarely tastes its food; instead it gulps it down. This is why it is easy for dogs to be poisoned, if the poison has no discernible odor. However, there are taste buds in the tongue and it is probable that the sense of taste is highly re-fined, and possibly used to supplement olfaction, in many cases.

The sense of touch is extremely important in very young pup-pies, who explore the environment with their muzzles and im-mediately start to suckle once they have encountered a teat. A dog sports sensitive whiskers (vibrissae) on either side of its muzzle. Otherwise, sensitive touch is severely restricted by the hard pads on their paws and the thick pelage of hair. However, dogs sense vibrations through their feet and possibly through the skin as well. Dogs are much more sensitive to electric shocks than humans, presumably because of the greater concentration of blood salts in dogs.

Sixth Sense?

Because of their "superior" intellectual functions, humans tend to project their awareness of the environment far beyond the realms of sensory perception. What they cannot see, hear, smell, taste or touch, they deduce . . . or imagine. The dog howeyer, is considerably more sensitive to a myriad of sounds and odors, to the extent that it enjoys a more complex sensory environment that is well beyond the capabilities of human perception. Perhaps a better understanding of the extent to which a dog may utilize its five senses may help to explain some curious phenomena that might otherwise be attributed to extrasensory perception.

There are some famous anecdotes about dogs' abilities to sense things that humans are unaware of. At first, these stories seem in-explicable on the basis that humans fail to comprehend them. They become classified as unaccountable phenomena that may be attributed to extrasensory perception, a sixth sense. From the dogs' point of view, things are usually much more simple; the ex-perience is not extrasensory, and there is no need to incorporate a sixth sense being used. Instead, the dog utilizes its existing five senses to a degree that humans have difficulty in appreciating, and fail to accept.

A classic example occurred in the home of an American military attache living in a foreign capital. One evening, the family dog began howling and whining and started scratching the floorboards in the corner of a room. The dog's master, thinking that the room was infested with mice or cockroaches, had the floorboards taken up, revealing a radio device which was transmitting the conversations in the room. The radio transmitter emitted a high-pitched whine, which although inaudible to humans, annoyed the dog. Neither extrasensory perception or a psychic phenomenon came into play; it was just plain old canine ultrasonics.

Other incidents that have been difficult to explain have involved the ability of some dogs to locate people buried in the snow and land mines hidden in the sand. Recent research has shown that the dog's nose contains infra-red receptors, which means that it is sensitive to temperature change. Perhaps a dog can sense the warmth of bodies in the snow or cold metal in the sand.

A dog can detect as little as one drop of blood in up to ten pints of water and can differentiate between salt solutions of magnesium sulphate and sodium sulphate. Perhaps such a nose is capable of actually smelling the metal of a buried land mine, in the same way that explosives, gas leaks and truffles can be located. It would seem that a dog has no particular need for a sixth sense, since it already has five perfectly good ones.

Everybody has heard one story or another about a happy family who moved from Pittsburgh to West Virginia, where they misplaced faithful, town-loving Rover the Rottweiler. The dog was presumed dead. . .until miraculously (being the most intelligent dog in the world) he turned up bedraggled, tired but trusty, at his old home in Pittsburgh, over one hundred miles away from West Virginia. There are many possible explanations for such incidents. With changes in latitude there are alterations in temperature, prevailing wind patterns and the angle of incidence of the midday sun, which a dog could use as a guide. Similarly, changes in longitude will cause an alteration in the time of sunrise and sunset, which will be out of phase with the dog's internal biological clock. (The dog has a very good sense of time and is remarkably successful in estimating the time of day. In an experiment, a dog was trained to ring a buzzer every one and a half minutes in order to receive a food reward. The dog performed the task with a high degree of accuracy). However, with a nose that can tell the difference between different salt solutions, a dog could probably smell Pittsburgh from two hundred miles away, let alone one hundred.

Such explanations are merely conjecture, but then the sensory world of animals is only barely understood, as attested by: the dolphin and bat radar; migration in insects, birds and fish; homing in pigeons; polaroid receptors in bees; infra-red receptors in pit vipers; and X-ray receptors in the olfactory bulbs of adult rats.

A final and well worn example is the case of a pet dog which manages to locate its owner several hundred miles away in a place the dog has never visited before. These examples are difficult to accurately document but in all probability they *do* occur. It would be a trifle presumptious to even attempt to interpret this one, but no doubt any dog could provide an obviously plausible and parsimonious explanation.

D-O-G SPELLS DOG: Canine Intelligence

Again I must remind you that
A dog's a dog— A cat's a cat . . .
T.S. Eliot (1939) "The Ad-Dressing of Cats."

One of the most commonly asked questions about animal intelligence is: "What is more intelligent: a cat or a dog?" Perhaps the greatest problem in assessing relative intelligence is devising a test which is equally suited for both parties. The difficulties lie in the establishment of non-biased terms of reference, or whether to make the comparison in terms of cat-intelligence or dog-intelligence. A cat would certainly excell in a complicated tree climbing test, whereas in a sheepherding competition a dog would no doubt be superior. Such comparisons are, of course, meaningless. A cat is not a dog. Cats and dogs have evolved so that they are best suited for their own particular ecological niche, and as we have seen in the preceding sections, the sensory and motor components of their behavior are similarly tailored so that they are relevant to this natural situation. Many so-called "intelligence" tests are dependent on sensory abilities, physique and past experiences. It would indeed be difficult to devise a test that would take all these factors into account.

Similar problems are encountered when attempting to measure breed differences in intelligence. There would be little point in comparing the performance of two breeds trained to retrieve an object from a table, if the dogs are a St. Bernard and a Chihuahua and the table is four feet high. A ridiculous example? Not really; some people are still intent on making such comparisons.

When considering different breeds, intelligence is often confused with *trainability*, which to some extent depends on the degree of *socialization* with humans. As a consequence, Foxhounds or Beagles, which normally have limited social contact with humans, are generally considered less intelligent than, for example, a Poodle. Often, owners will make up their minds in advance that some breeds, such as terriers, are untrainable, and this is then accepted as a valid excuse for not even bothering to try. On the other hand, the owner of a thousand dollar Chesapeake Bay Retriever is convinced beforehand that the dog is capable of the most outstanding canine feats.

An alternative approach has been to consider the intelligence of cats and dogs in terms of human intelligence. This comparison is equally meaningless and has an unpleasant touch of anthropocentric chauvinism. Cats and dogs are not humans. Rather than involving the solution of various man-made problems, which an animal would certainly never encounter in its natural surroundings, the intelligence of dogs should be measured (if at all) in terms of their ability to adapt to and make the most of their immediate physical and social environment.

At a southern college in the United States, an experiment was designed to measure the maze learning performance of white rats and college sophomores; the latter traced the maze with their fingers. The rats learned the maze three times faster than the college students. Surely, one would not interpret these findings by suggesting that white rats are more intelligent than college sophomores. A college sophomore's fingers are not used to maze running; the student has little adaptive value for such. For rats, however, it bears some direct relation to their natural habitat. Rats live in mazes, and rapid maze learning is an extremely adaptive trait. It would obviously be unfair to measure human intelligence in rat terms, and similarly there is little value in measuring animal intelligence in human terms.

Do Dogs Think?
Artistotle said that the main difference between humans and

animals was that, although animals can learn and remember, only humans were capable of reason. Since the time of Aristotle, the question whether or not animals can reason has been, and still is, a heated debate. A number of investigators have worked with apes, trying to demonstrate examples of deductive reasoning. Some workers emphatically deny that any non-human animals are capable of reasoning, whereas others, including the popular press and a large majority of pet owners armed with a regiment of anecdotes, subscribe to the contrary. It is true that there is an outstanding difference between the reasoning powers of humans and animals but this may reflect a considerable quantitative difference rather than a qualitative one. This difference is probably due to language, which is certainly the greatest distinction between animals and humans. The written and spoken word is certainly an extremely efficient means for human thought, reason and communication. It has been shown that individual apes may learn sign language and are capable of mastering a large vocabulary, part of which involves word concepts, but obviously this would not occur under normal conditions in their natural environment. Similarly, in 1928 there was a German Shepherd Dog named Fellow that had learned the meaning of 500 words, and understood at least 200 different verbal commands. However, it is unlikely that animals could have learned these words on their own, since the acquisition of even a modest vocabulary required intensive human tuition. Nevertheless, it does indicate that they do have some capacity for learning the human language. But here again, this is an unfair and meaningless comparision, since animals have their own language and means to communicate. How much of the canine language have humans even bothered to learn? Very little indeed!

Although there is little evidence to suggest that dogs do think or reason, it is also impossible to say that they do not. Nevertheless, they probably lack the complex symbolism and sophisticated concepts that are involved in human language. It would be a very intangible and abstract thought, without any words, which is as difficult to imagine as it is to describe. It would be a rudimentary thinking of sensory impressions and feelings with perhaps some elementary canine symbolism of tail wags and ear positions. Although it is now accepted that the animal mind is very different from the "animal machines" of Descartes' mechanistic theory,

Cartoonist Murray Ball has humorously explored the subtle differences between the reasoning powers of dogs and humans.

Punch Magazine, November 28, 1973.

there is still no need to revert to confusing and unwarranted anthropomorphisms.

For some inexplicable reason, when a dog learns to open a door to come inside, or a cupboard to get food, these acts are often viewed as evidence of sophisticated reasoning or even the deliberate imitation of humans. It would be a trifle hasty to assume such a simple deed as indication of superior intellectual functioning; instead it would be more pertinent to attempt to discover how the dog learned its little tricks.

One of the greatest American psychologists, Edward Lee Thorndike, designed several problem boxes for cats, dogs and chickens to determine whether animals employed reasoning when attempting to solve a puzzle. The animal was put inside a box which had a door that could be opened from the inside by pressing a lever, pulling a cord or even working a thumb latch. When a dog was introduced into the problem box, it would indiscriminately bite and claw everything in sight. Via this assault on the apparatus, the dog would eventually be accidently successful in effecting its escape and was rewarded with a little food for its effort. If dogs were capable of reasoning, it would be expected that in future trials, they would open the door much quicker now that the solution had been discovered. However, when the dog was reintroduced into the problem box, there was no significant change in its technique. It would still go through the entire repertoire of escape movements, and there was little, if any, reduction in the escape time. One must assume that although the dog was trying to escape, it had no specific *intention* to open the door. On further attempts, the same sequence of events occurred and it was only after a great number of trials that there was any reduction in the escape time. Following the first accidental success, as the task was repeated there was a gradual elimination of irrelevant behaviors, until all that remained was the effective escape response. Even at this stage, it is difficult to say whether the animal has recognized the solution to the problem that by pressing a lever, the door will open; or whether it is still executing a stereotyped and shortened version of the original repertoire of escape behavior to which the door opens incidentally. There was no evidence to suggest that the problems were solved by reasoning or sudden insight. The dogs' approach was very different from the deliberate trial and error method that a child might employ, in which subsequent trials are substantially shorter.

The escape time was not significantly shortened by allowing the dog to watch humans or other animals solve the problem. Even trying to instruct the animal by placing its paw on the lever and pushing down, had no significant effect on escape times. It seems highly unlikely that dogs are able to learn the solution by *rational* imitation. In the wild, it is probable that one animal may learn by imitating another, but this is certainly not a rational process. Instead, the young may simply follow adult animals and gradually go through the process of performing, practicing and perfecting various behavior patterns.

Anecdotes

The majority of evidence in support of a lofty canine intellect comes mainly from a battery of anecdotes and cute doggy stories, often with the family pet starring in the main role. This is not to belittle such observations, since a good deal of useful information has come from accurate observation. However, the main objection to many of these examples, upon which grandiose assumptions have been based, is that they are not *respresentative* of the entire behavioral repertoire of the dog. Instead, they are merely isolated examples which may be few and far between. As such, they are difficult to interpret, since often the preceding history is unknown, or at best obscure, and there is seldom any control over the infinite number of variables that could have influenced the outcome. The non-representative nature of these isolated examples has been summed up by a famous American psychologist, T.C. Schneirla, when he wrote that "one who sets out to demonstrate that protozoan organisms or any others have the mental characteristics of man may convince himself at least, provided he singles out opportunely the brief episodes which seem desirable as instances of perception, of danger, of reasoning or what not. By the same method, the absence of reasoning in man can be proved with ease."

Despite this, many dog owners, breeders and trainers continually attach great importance to those occasional instances, which are interpreted as true examples of reasoning or other intelligent behavior.

56

In the same way that it requires training to become a legal secretary, brain surgeon or mechanic, it takes a certain amount of experience to learn how to reliably observe animal behavior. Usually, doggy anecdotes are recounted by untrained observers, and they may consequently be liable to error. Even a trained observer exerts some bias, especially if a "pet" theory is at stake. Even in those cases where the observation has been an accurate account of what happened, more unreliable is the interpretation of the facts at hand. It is often difficult to be completely objective when considering such accounts, and one is especially biased when considering one's own pet dog. This bias need not necessarily be intentional, but instead the interpretation may be unconsciously guided by the simple fact that one's own pet pooch is the most intelligent and brightest star that has ever coursed the heavens.

There may be a variety of explanations for any given situation, and it is impossible to say for certain which is correct. For example, consider a dog owner who returns home to find out the waste paper basket had been overturned and our amazingly intelligent canine friend had relieved itself right in the middle of the papers that were strewn on the floor. The owner may assume that the dog surprised itself with a full rectum and knowing that it could not get out of the house, cleverly reasoned that it would find some paper to protect the Navajo rug from fecal contamination and thus avert the owner's distress and financial ruin. Lloyd Morgan, an English animal behaviorist, proposed a "Law of Parsimony" (Morgan's Canon), which stated that one should not interpret a behavior as the outcome of a higher mental process if it may be adequately explained as the product of some mental process on a lower scale. That is to say, when there are several interpretations available, the simplest and most parsimonious explanation is often preferred. Nonetheless, the simplest answers need not be the correct ones, and may not reflect the entire explanation of a more complicated problem. However, what could be an alternative explanation for the above example? Perhaps the dog inadvertently knocked over the waste basket while playing . . . perhaps it had been paper trained as a puppy and the combined stimulus of feces in rectum and paper under paws caused the dog to defecate. A great many perhaps, but then that's the trouble with anecdotes.

In the same way that many people are anthropocentric in their insistence of assessing intelligence in dogs on the basis of problem solving and reasoning, they are equally anthropomorphic in the interpretation of their observations. One of the most common misconceptions is to assume that because a dog has performed a particular act, it necessarily thought about it beforehand. Here, of course, there is the classic example of Hans, the clever horse, which was owned by Herr von Osten in Berlin around 1901. Hans could solve fairly complicated mathematical problems, which were written on the blackboard, and Hans would stamp out the answer with his hoof. Hans was not infallible. He would sometimes make the occasional error (don't we all) but the percentage of correct responses was truly amazing, and many people were convinced of Hans' outstanding equine intellect. However, it was found that whenever Herr von Osten was absent during the testing period, Hans would be incapable of solving even the simplest of problems. Instead, he would continue stamping far beyond the correct answer of the problem. It seemed that Hans was not so clever after all. He had simply learned to commence tapping when the problem was presented on the blackboard and to stop tapping in response to some slight involuntary signal given by the owner. One must presume that Herr von Osten was not a con artist; instead he was understandably anxious for Hans to succeed and was extremely tense during the performance. As soon as Hans had given the correct number of taps, Herr von Osten would show very slight signs of relief, which Hans was capable of perceiving.

Similar instances frequently occur during dog trials. Often, when a dog has made a mistake and jumped over the wrong fence, it responds immediately by sitting down. At the time this occurs, in the limelight of the public eye, the owner is usually in a state of frustrated fury. The dog is subsequently forgiven for making a fool of itself and its owner, who now considers the dog to be highly intelligent, since it realized that it had made a mistake. Another explanation might be that after making the error, the dog perceives slight changes in the owner's behavior, which might range from mild exasperation to a maniacal fury. When the owner is annoyed, the dog's first response is to sit down, since this is most likely the first command it was taught. In the above situa-

58

Why did this dog climb a tree? Those who would attribute powers of reason to dogs might say that she climbed the tree to get a better view.

tion, there is no need to implicate remarkable reasoning powers, or even doggy guilt and conscience; instead, the dog is simply given an elementary response to a cue from its owner. The reason for the misinterpretation is the fact that these simple cues are often imperceptible to humans.

Consider two final examples of a dog that could operate a food vending machine. Truly impressive! The dog had been trained to press a lever on the side of a box in order to receive a dog biscuit that was dispensed in a food chute. However, if the box was rotated through 90 degrees, the dog would continue to make pawing motions on the side of the box where the lever *used* to be, although the lever was in full view only a few inches away. The important fact here is that the dog had not learned to press a lever for a food reward, but instead it had been trained to make pawing movements at a particular point in space. The dog was relying on quite different senses than a human would in attempting the problem. To the dog, the precise location of the pawing movements was more important than the actual lever. It took several trials with the vending machine in a variety of positions before the dog learned that the lever was the key to dog biscuit nirvana.

A similar example is offered by dogs that were trained to pick up a ball from a tray and drop it in a hole in the counter, which was situated eight inches to the left of the tray, in order to receive a food reward. If the counter was moved so that it was situated eight inches to the right of the tray, the dog would pick up a ball and carry it eight inches to the *left*, as before, and drop it in midair 16 inches from the counter. At this stage in the learning process, the dog had not yet learned that in order to get a food reward it must drop the ball through the hole. It had simply learned to pick up a ball and carry it a certain distance in a certain direction before dropping it. Again, the dog was affording greater importance to different sensory modalities than those which a human might use. The relative position of the objects was of more pertinence to the dog, which therefore relied to a great extent upon kinaesthetic and proprioceptive senses. On first impressions, a dog working a food vending machine seemed pretty impressive, but a closer examination of the learning process reveals a much more stereotyped set of behavior patterns, which are dependent on an entirely different set of environmental cues. A dog dropping a ball in a hole which is not there might seem pretty dumb to a human, but then a human getting lost in a forest might seem equally dumb to a dog, if only it had adequate mental faculty to reflect on the matter.

3. Canine Communication

The preceding chapter alluded that dogs have a language of their own. In fact, they have several, relying on a variety of senses. The method of communication employed depends largely on the distance between the two animals. In close proximity, they are likely to employ all three types: body postures and facial expressions, vocalizations and an exchange of odors. When not in visual contact, vocalizations serve an important function for locating animals over large distances. With olfactory communication, there is an added advantage. One dog may lay down a scent mark which will last for several days and the marker may be miles away before the message is discovered by another dog.

VISUAL COMMUNICATION

Body Language

A large number of dogs' facial gestures and bodily postures are indicative of their intentions and emotional state. Some are rather gross signs that are patently obvious even to a human observer. Others are more subtle, both in their execution and meaning, and of course, perhaps there are some signals which we humans fail to notice altogether. The repertoire of body language is comparatively uniform throughout all members of the canine family. It has been suggested that the more social the species, the more sophisticated the system of visual communication employed in social interactions. Thus, pack-living species like the wolf would have a more sophisticated repertoire of visual signals than the semi-solitary pair-bonding jackals and coyotes, or solitary species such as the red fox and Arctic fox. However, there are many exceptions to this rule. It is difficult to accurately assess where domestic dogs fit into this framework, largely because of considerable breed differences. Some breeds are limited in their expression; a number have long pendulous ears; others have had their ears clipped so that they stand erect and are capable of very little movement; other breeds are docked, having no tails to wag.

Face. The facial musculature of the dog is capable of a number of expressions. There does not appear to be the variety of facial expressions that occur in humans, but with dogs even subtle changes are very much accentuated by the characteristic facial markings. In addition, the position of the ears and tail, along with general bodily posture, appear to serve important communicatory functions.

Mouth. A slightly open mouth with bared teeth is usually indicative of a threat. The corners of the mouth are pulled forward and the upper lip is lifted to expose the canines. In the so-called "submissive grin," the corners of the mouth are pulled back, in-

A high ranking dog is "staring down" a lower ranking animal, which will soon retreat to a safer distance.

dicating insecurity or subordination. The lips may be held together or occasionally slightly parted and the tip of the tongue may be extruded as if making licking motions.

Ears. When the animal is alert, the ears are normally erect and both pointing forward. This is the sign of a confident dog, whether it is friendly or aggressive. As the dog becomes more anxious or fearful, the ears are turned down and point backwards, and in a fearful threat they lie completely flattened against the back of the head.

Tail. The main difference between the tail positions of dogs and wolves is that a dog has a naturally curly tail, and the straight tail positions commonly seen in wolves are much rarer in domestic dogs. Some breeds of dogs have their tails docked as part of breed requirements, such as the Doberman Pinscher. Others have permanently coiled tails, such as the Spitz and Samoyed.

The tail may vary in both position and movement. Characteristically, the tail of a dominant dog is held high, whereas the tail of a subordinate is lowered and may be tucked between the hind legs. As a generalization, this holds true, but there are, of course, many exceptions. There are two common tail positions of a confident, relaxed dog. During social interactions or while walking and actively exploring the environment, the tail is normally held in a curled position above the horizontal and often wagged briskly from side to side. If the dog stops to eat or to investigate an odor, the tail will gradually drop to a relaxed curled position below the horizontal. Usually the wagging ceases and the tail is held stationary, sometimes hanging loosely and pointing straight down.

In threatening situations, the tail is usually held high. It may be perpendicular or curled over the back. As the tension of the situation increases, the tail may become more rigid. In some cases, the tip of the tail appears to be trembling or vibrating with an extremely high frequency, low amplitude wag. Often this will happen when two dogs of similar status are threatening each other. In such disputes, the outcome is often uncertain and the participants seem involved in an intricate game of bluff.

A tail tucked between the legs is indicative of a dog that is insecure or uncertain. This often occurs following a threatening situation or social imbroglio with an animal of higher status. During active appeasement, when a subordinate is approaching a superior, the tail is characteristically held in this position. Although the tail may be held quite stationary, the hindquarters appear to wag from side to side.

There is one position of the tail that characterizes a bitch when she is in heat. The tail is deviated to one side, so as to expose the vulvar region, and periodically it may flap from side to side like a metronome. Tail deviations normally occur in response to mounting by a prospective mate, or occasionally following an investigation of the bitch by a suitor. At the height of estrus, the tail may deviate spontaneously at the mere sight of a male.

Body. As a general rule, when a dog is bluffing or threatening, the various bodily postures tend to make it look large and imposing; whereas, when appeasing, it appears to look much smaller. In the typical threat posture, the dog stands squarely on all four legs with the head held high and tail and ears erect, usually staring directly towards its opponent. Sometimes there is a piloerection of the hairs along the scruff of the neck and down the ridge of the back. As the animal approaches, it walks slowly with a rigid, purposeful gait. If a dog is threatening out of fear, the head is usually slightly lowered and the ears are flattened against the head, the tail hangs in a curve below the horizontal and is slowly brushed from side to side. These are signs to watch out for. The dog is afraid, and if approached too closely will often bite in self-defense.

When showing signs of appeasement or submission, the head and forequarters are held low, the ears lie flat against the head, and the tail is tucked between the legs. The body seems to slink along with the abdomen almost in contact with the ground, and the entire rear wags from side to side. The dog may lie down on its side and lift one leg so as to expose its anal and genital regions. In extreme cases, the dog will roll over on its back and urinate, which must be considered the ultimate sign of deference.

In the play-soliciting posture, the front half of the body is lowered with the front paws, elbows and sternum in contact with the ground while the rump is prominently stuck in the air with the tail wagging furiously. The dog may characteristically prance in this position, occasionally barking and often it will make pawing motions towards the other dog.

Juvenile males approach an adult male that has possession of a bone. Not quite sure how the dog in the ditch may react, they approach somewhat cautiously.

AUDITORY COMMUNICATION
Vocalizations: Whimpers, Growls, Barks and Howls

Wolf vocalizations have been characteristically divided into four basic categories; the whimper, the bark, the howl and the growl. They appear to be identical to those observed in dogs. It is extremely difficult to estimate how efficient these sounds are in conveying information. The four types of vocalizations are quite distinct, and all appear to have separate meanings. However, it is highly probable that dogs are capable of interpreting far more from the sounds than meets the human ear.

Whimpers and Whines. There are two puppy vocalizations which should be considered in this section, mewing and whining. The very first sound that a puppy is able to make is a soft mewing sound, which it makes during times of stress: when it is uncomfortable, hungry, cold or in pain. It serves much the same function as the cry of a human baby. As the puppy grows older, instead of indiscriminate mewing sounds, the dog's distress calls become more explicit: whines, whimpers and yelps. Domestic dogs are much more apt to whine than wolves. The increased tendency to whine in the domestic situation is largely due to unintentional encouragement by owners, so that the indiscriminate mewing of puppyhood persists in the form of equally indiscriminate whining. For example, consider a dog that is sitting in the cold and rain and incessantly whining and scratching at the door. After some period of time the owner grudgingly leaves the warmth of a fireside armchair, ostensibly to let the dog inside but in reality to stop the whining. For the owner the problem has been solved, at least for the present. But the dog has achieved the desired result and will consequently be more likely to whine in similar situations in the future. After no time at all, the dog will start to whine in any and every slightly stressful situation as long as the owner continues to aid and abet the habit.

Perhaps the only evidence of whining in adult wolves is the whimper of a subordinate animal, usually as an appeasement gesture when threatened. The sound is very similar to a whine but of much shorter duration. Other vocalizations that have been reported are the "social squeak," an extremely soft sound supposedly uttered during social encounters, and the yelp, a short high pitched squeak which is emitted when the dog has experienced a sudden pain, such as a bee sting or a clumsy boot on the paw.

Growls. Whereas whimpers and whines are an indication of need or friendly subordination, growling usually constitutes a threat, signifying antagonistic intentions. The majority of dogs usually give plenty of warning before they attack. They may stare, growl, snarl and perhaps snap a few times before they will actually initiate a fight.

Barks. The majority of breeds of domestic dog bark more frequently than wolves. It has been suggested that for wolves the bark serves a variety of functions: the call of the chase, a threat and an alarm call. In domestic dogs, the bark probably serves similar functions. There is a considerable breed difference in the degree of barking. A Basenji, the "barkless dog," will seldom bark more than once or twice in a session, whereas a Cocker Spaniel will usually bark fifteen or twenty times before stopping. During the process of domestication, it would seem that the propensity to bark has been strongly selected for, perhaps because of the dog's early function as a shepherd dog or watch dog, where the barking was a successful deterrent to would-be intruders.

Domestic dogs bark in most any situation where they have become excited, usually when there is some new activity that is worthy of mention. The barks are short and sharp, which facilitates the location of the barker. The dog seems to be saying: "dog here. . . I know something is going on. . . wait for further communication." In domestic life the dog tends to use the bark much like the whine, as auditory blackmail to get what it wants from its owners; the bark has become more of a generalized call for attention. Occasionally, a hoarse guttural bark may be used as a low grade threat, in which case it almost borders on an explosive growl, (more like a "grrrwoof").

Howls. In general, howling is more common in wolves than in domestic dogs. However, some breeds, such as the Northern dogs, (Malamutes, Huskies) howl quite frequently and of course Beagles are renowned for their bugling.

Howling in wolves is a complicated sound. Spectographic analysis has revealed that it consists of a fundamental frequency with as many as twelve harmonically related overtones. It has been found that each animal howls quite distinctively from others, which would seem to suggest the possibility that individuals may be recognized by their howling. Also, there are variations within the howling repertoire of each individual. It has long been assumed that howling serves as an advertisement of territory allowing adequate spacing between packs and individuals. However, different howls may have different meanings and it has been claimed, for instance, that it is possible to distinguish howls of loneliness from howls after feeding in captive wolves. In addition, it has been suggested that howling is the call of the chase. This may be the case with domestic dogs, and several breeds of hounds and hunting dogs have been bred to bark or howl once they have picked up a scent or treed a raccoon. However, wolves tend to be quiet while hunting, and howling is probably more important in assembling the pack after the hunt.

Whatever the function of howling, it is certainly true that it is a communal affair in both wolves and domestic dogs. Once a wolf begins howling, others eagerly run to join in and the general atmosphere appears to be one of enthusiasm and excitement. Howling seems to serve an important social function, a happy community occasion where the wolves may congregate for an enjoyable singsong. Dogs also show a strong tendency to join in once an individual has started howling. This is particularly evident in a pack of hounds, but even dogs living in separate households are eager to join in the chorus that was triggered by a single dog.

OLFACTORY COMMUNICATION

In man, social intercourse has centered mainly on the process of absorbing fluid into the organism, but in the domestic dog and to a lesser extent among all wild canine species, the act charged with most social significance is the excretion of fluid. For man the pub, the estaminet, the Biergarten, but for the dog the treetrunk, the lintel of door or gate, and above all the lamppost, form the focal points of community life. For a man the flavors of alcoholic drinks, but for a dog the infinitely variegated smells of urine are the most potent stimuli for the gregarious impulse.

From *The Lamppost, A Study of the Social Life of the Domestic Dog* by Sirius (quoted in *Sirius* by Olaf Stapledon)

Many dog owners have realized that their pets urinate with a frequency that seems far in excess of their normal metabolic need. It has been surmised that urination serves functions other than just the elimination of urine, especially since the majority of urinations are preceded by a great deal of olfactory investigation of the surroundings. Most dog owners are similarly aware that when two dogs meet they proceed to "sniff each other out." There is sometimes a brief contact of muzzles followed by a mutual anal and genital investigation, depending on how well the dogs are acquainted. During this fleeting olfactory encounter a great deal of information is exchanged between the two dogs. There are many potential sources of communicative odors in the dog: urine, vaginal secretions, feces, anal gland secretions, saliva and a variety of other bodily secretions.

68

Most dogs will thoroughly investigate the area before urinating.

Dogs will often approach another dog that is urinating.

Some dogs will scratch the ground after elimination.

Urination, aside from being an obviously vital body function, is used as a method of communication, and as a means of territory demarcation.

Urine. Of all the potential odor sources, urine appears to be the most important as far as communication is concerned. This would seem to make sense, if only because of the sheer frequency with which dogs urinate and investigate the urine of other dogs. A dog may acquire considerable information about other dogs by sniffing only a drop of their urine. It may ascertain the sex of the individual, whether or not a male has been castrated, or, in the case of a female, spayed. Perhaps more importantly, (for male dogs at least), they may tell whether female urine came from an anestrous bitch or from one in heat. Anybody who has owned a bitch becomes aware, when she comes into heat, that they unwittingly entertain all the male dogs in the neighborhood, the majority of which scratch at doors and fences, barking, whining, urinating on the lawn, digging up gladioli, defecating on the petunias and otherwise making a general nuisance of themselves. And of course this is only half of the problem. The bitch is usually just as determined to entertain her prospective suitors, and should she manage a quick bit of the old one-two, the result is unwanted puppies.

What exactly is it that attracts the males from afar?

Of course it's mostly the luscious smell of her. I can't possibly make you understand the power of it, because you humans are so bad at smells. It's as though your noses are not merely feeble but color blind. But think of all that your poets have ever said about the delectable curves and colors of the beloved, and how her appearance seems to express a lovely *spirit* (often deceptively), and then imagine the whole thing done in terms of fragrance. Morwens' fragance when she wants me is like the scent of the morning, with a maddening tang in it for which there are no words. It is like the scent of a very gentle and fragrant *spirit*.

from Sirius

When a bitch is in heat, not only is her urine extremely attractive to male dogs, but during that time she is apt to wander over larger distances and urinate much more frequently on her travels. As a result, she leaves an open urinary invitation to any and every male dog in the vicinity, in the form of a series of odor trails which converge at her place of residence. Once the prospective mates have met each other there often follows a sequence of urinary behavior, whereby one animal urinates and the other animal investigates the urine and then urinates itself, only to be followed by a prompt investigation and perhaps additional urination on behalf of the original dog. Both the attractiveness of urine of the opposite sex and perhaps the entire sequence of urinary behavior itself seem to excite both partners and stimulate further courtship behaviors, eventually culminating in mating.

It would seem that in domestic dogs the principal function of urinary scent marking is sexual attraction. However, there has been a lot of speculation that one function of urinary scent marking is the demarcation of territory. This may be true, but there is no evidence to suggest that domestic dogs are respectors of territory, whether it is marked or unmarked. Contrarily, domestic dogs are notorious for roaming over a large area and normally show little regard for so-called territorial boundaries. Somehow, the notion has crept into literature that all dogs are strictly territorial, and that each dog daily patrols the perimeter of its territory, conscientiously marking at regular intervals. It is certainly true that dogs, particularly males, will urinate against almost any prominent visual or olfactory landmark. This is especially true if

Above: Adult males elevate a hind leg and usually direct the urine towards a vertical object. Below: A male puppy stands on all four legs and leans forward when urinating.

A bitch, above, squats when urinating. Below: A female puppy will also squat when urinating.

they are kept inside for the majority of the day and only allowed outside for short walks. In such cases, it would not be unusual for a dog to urinate dozens of times in a few minutes. However, it would seem unlikely that domestic dogs, or wolves, for that matter, are strictly territorial animals. A territory is a protected area that is defended against intruders. Domestic dogs will wander freely through each other's territories, and with wolves, their home range is so extensive that it would be impossible for any pack to adequately defend it against all intruders. Usually, only that area immediately surrounding the den will be defended, particularly if cubs are present.

Nevertheless, domestic dogs have had artificial territories created for them by apartment walls and garden fences. Depending on the personality of the individual dog, some will protect these artificial, small territories, especially if other dogs have never been allowed inside. A dog may soon develop an equally artificial bravado towards all potential intruders, canine or human. The dog may bark and growl to its heart's content, secure in the knowledge that it is unable to get out, or perhaps more to the point, that the other dog is unable to get in.

So, what is the reason for all this urinating? Perhaps dogs feel more comfortable if the environment has been daubed with the familiarity of their own odors. Thus, in order to preserve its individual homey smell, a dog is likely to urinate on any intruding odor, such as that of another dog's feces. Similarly, when humans move house, the new residence is usually decorated with familiar furniture and wallhangings. . .and it soon takes on the appearance of home.

Male dogs urinate more frequently than bitches do, but urine marking is not the sole prerogative of the male. However, compared with females, males do spend more time investigating the surroundings before urinating and are much more likely to orient their urine toward conspicuous objects such as a tree, lamppost, or fire hydrant. Also, dogs will orient their urinations toward prominent olfactory landmarks, perhaps to accentuate their signature. Often, a male will start to lift one leg and then lift the other, repeating the process several times before actually urinating. During this orienting behavior, it is common for the dog to repeatedly sniff the potential urination target. Some dogs may growl when

Most dogs defecate using the same characteristic posture. The spine is arched and the hind legs are plantigrade and splayed out at "ten to two."

they encounter urine from strange males. After urinating in the open, it is not uncommon for a dog to vigorously scratch the ground, so as to provide an additional visual cue to draw attention to the odor. This particular behavior is quite the contrary to that of cats who, after elimination, bury their waste.

For the male dog, estrous vaginal secretions provide an additional source of attraction and offer another means by which male dogs can determine whether a female is in heat.

Feces. Dogs are also particular about where they defecate. Each defecation is usually preceded by a thorough investigation of the area, whereupon the dog will characteristically embark on a peculiar circling behavior before actually defecating. Some dogs will employ more unusual postures in order to place the feces on vertical targets. It would seem that feces also has some importance in olfactory communication, and it is known that following an investigation of fecal deposits, male dogs are able to identify the sex of the defecator.

Anal glands. The function of anal glands still remains much of a mystery. For a long time it was thought that anal sac secretions served as a deterrent. When dogs are frightened or excited they are capable of squirting the secretions up to a distance of two or three

It is quite normal for females to raise a leg when urinating. However, this posture is quite different from the adult male leg elevation posture. Below: On occasions unusual postures may be used when defecating. This male is employing the characteristic urination posture.

Above, the highest ranking male puppy stands over and growls at a low ranking male, which has submissively rolled onto its side. Below, the lower ranking male attempts to retreat but is mounted by the top-dog. A high ranking individual will normally not permit mounting from inferiors in the social hierarchy.

yards, much like a skunk. Also, it has been suggested that female anal sac secretions become more attractive as a bitch comes into heat. This is unlikely, and although anal sac secretions come in a wide variety of odors, colors and consistencies, the particular type of secretion bears no relation to the dog's sex or hormonal status. However, it does appear that dogs have their own unique brand of secretion, and perhaps they are individualized in much the same way as a human thumb print or a gorilla's nose print.

Saliva. When dogs greet each other they often sniff and lick each others' muzzles. By so doing, they might discover whether the other dog had eaten recently.

Elimination Postures. Since the latter part of this chapter has mainly concerned the rear end of the dog, we may as well round it off by saying a few words about urination and defecation postures. It is generally accepted that when a male dog urinates, it lifts one leg and directs the urine towards some vertical surface, whereas a female simply squats and urinates on the ground. It has been assumed that a bitch urinates merely out of physiological necessity and that the important social function of urinary scent marking is reserved for males.

The assumptions about male urinations are largely correct. In the vast majority of male urinations, a hind leg is lifted so that the urine may be directed towards a prominent vertical landmark, such as a tree or fence. Occasionally, males may urinate in the open, but they still tend to lift their legs to some degree. Immature males urinate in a standing position. The hind legs are held straight, although in some cases they are slightly flexed, so that the dog leans forward slightly and the back slopes downwards towards the rear.

Some male dogs have a leg preference when urinating and will orient their bodies accordingly. Others are ambipedal (may lift either leg). On occasion, male dogs may revert to the juvenile urination posture. This sometimes occurs when they urinate in the open and it is comparatively common if the dog is sick.

The assumptions about female urinary behavior are not entirely correct. Many dog owners are apt to worry when they observe that their bitch raises a leg while urinating. This behavior, however, is common and may be considered as being quite normal. In fact, over 25 per cent of all females will raise one leg or the other when urinating. Nevertheless, with females the leg is raised in a manner which is quite different from the normal leg elevation in males. The male abducts the limb so that it is rotated outwards and upwards to lie in a flexed position above the horizontal plane of the back. The dog balances on the other hind leg, which usually remains fully extended. In this manner, the underside of the body becomes aligned laterally and the urine is dispersed in that direction. When a female raises her leg, it is often flexed and brought forward off the ground so that it remains below the horizontal plane of the body and the flow of urine is directed downwards and not laterally. The other leg is usually flexed to varying degrees so that the female appears to be in a squatting position with one leg raised. Only in very rare circumstances have females been seen to employ the full leg elevation posture that is characteristic of the male.

Compared to males, females display a greater selection of urination postures. Particular postures are often dictated by the environmental setting. When a female urinates simply out of the need to relieve herself, she will usually squat. However, when urinating in response to a previous urine mark, she is likely to use a posture which engineers the flow of urine as close to the desired spot as possible. Occasionally, this may take the form of a rather bizarre hand-stand posture, in which both hind legs may be supported against a vertical surface and it appears that the dog walks up the wall backwards. This type of posture has also been observed in female bushdogs and a similar unsupported hand-stand has been seen in courting male Cape hunting dogs.

The sexually dimorphic urination postures presumably have communicative values, since from a distance an observing dog may determine the sex of the other animal. This is especially the case with male dogs, in which a hind leg is elevated much like a flag, as if to indicate the dog's maleness and the fact that it is urinating. It is quite common for other dogs to approach from afar to investigate the urine.

Whether or not a dog will employ the leg elevating posture during adulthood is determined very early in its development. Exposure to testosterone from the fetal testes seems to preprogram the development of the male pattern of urination at a later date. Male dogs normally commence lifting their legs at puberty. However, strangely enough the manifestation of this behavior seems to have very little to do with the levels of testosterone in the blood at that time. In fact, a dog that has been castrated well before the onset of puberty will still commence leg elevating at approximately the same time as intact males. Why then do some females raise their legs? Perhaps they have been exposed to low levels of the male sex hormone, testosterone from their brother womb mates *in utero*, or perhaps their mother's adrenals, or even their own, produced small levels of androgens.

The majority of dogs, whether male or female, defecate using the same characteristic posture. The hind legs are flexed and the feet are splayed out at "ten to two." Also, the spine is arched so that the anal region is close to and directed toward the ground. Again however, there may be variations. Females may raise one leg, and on rare occasions males may even defecate in the full leg elevation posture. This may occur when the animal defecates immediately after urinating. Some dogs may employ the handstand posture for defecations, in order to place the feces on a vertical target. Although the majority of defecations occur in the open, more than a quarter are directed toward vertical targets. Following defecation, some dogs will scratch the ground and provide an additional visual landmark to further advertise the deposit. Other dogs may bark while defecating, as if to say "I'm doing it, come and have a sniff."

A peculiar canine behavior is the habit of rolling in strong-smelling substances, such as feces or decaying carcasses. If the dog is rolling in its own feces, this might represent a mechanism whereby the animal is further accentuating the scent of the dog, which might be important during social or sexual encounters. However, both bovine and equine feces seem to be favorite choices, and it has been suggested that this type of behavior developed for quite the opposite purpose, to disguise the dogs' odor while in foreign territory. After all, what better way to hunt wild ungulates than when smartly attired in a splendid accoutrement of bovine feces?

4. Social Behavior

SOCIAL SYSTEMS OF WILD CANIDAE

Pet owners are aware of numerous differences between the behavior of cats and dogs. These specific observations of two domestic species reflect overall differences between the social behavior of members of the dog and cat families. To a large extent, the social organization of carnivores is directly related to two prime factors: their hunting methods and the availability of prey, and the stability of their reproductive relationship.

Members of the cat family are solitary animals and generally only come together at mating times. An exception to this is the lion, which represents the only truly social felid. Cats tend to hunt individually, and the prey may be of equal size to themselves. Often they will lie in wait for likely prey, then a protracted stealthy approach is followed by a rapid pounce. Often, the kill is a quick one, the result of a crushed skull or neck. Sometimes the neck bite is less severe, and the prey will die slowly from suffocation while the cat lies on top of it. As a rule, cats have an extremely specialized diet and are almost entirely carnivorous.

In contrast, members of the dog family display a wide variety of diets, hunting methods and reproductive strategies. As a consequence, there is considerable variation in the types of social organization within the dog family. Compared with a cat, a dog's diet is varied. One reason for this may be that dogs are not arboreal, and therefore animal prey is more limited. As a result, they employ a number of appropriate hunting methods to exploit a variety of alternative food sources. They will eat invertebrates, such as slugs and snails, which require very little hunting expertise, small rodents, which they will pounce on in the same manner as a cat will, or larger herbivores which they will usually run down after a lengthy chase. Small prey are usually killed fairly quickly by a head shake, which either breaks or crushes the neck, whereas larger prey usually weaken and die following repeated bites, after which they are eviscerated during a pack feed.

The particular hunting strategy is largely dictated by the prevailing food conditions. Pack-living wolves have been known to eke out a scavenging existence in order to compensate for adverse conditions. When prey is scarce, a wolf's diet may consist of fruits and vegetables, carrion, and other items that may be scavenged.

Some wild dogs, such as dingoes, live a mainly solitary existence much like members of the cat family, and only come together for mating, after which the male customarily departs, leaving the female to raise the litter on her own. Other canids, although primarily living separately, will remain together in a temporary pair bond following the mating period. It is easier for two parents to raise the litter than just one, and the extra parental help also allows for larger litter sizes. This situation has additional advantages: a pair of jackals hunting together is considerably more successful than the collective efforts of the two hunting separately. For this and other reasons, once a pair has come together for breeding purposes, they may continue their pair bonding relationship on a permanent basis. Such is the case with many foxes. Often, once a male red fox has mated with a vixen, he will not mate with another female.

There are three wild canids that normally live in packs: the wolf, the Cape hunting dog and the dhole (a fierce wild dog). Cooperative group hunting makes it easier to run down prey and also allows the pack to kill animals that are larger than themselves.

A pack probably arises from a pair and their pups, rather than from a congregation of unrelated individuals. Once formed, a pack offers significant advantages. It is easier to locate and hunt food; during the breeding season it is not necessary to go in search of a mate; there are more individuals to help care for and feed the pups and be on the alert and defend against intruders and potential predators. However, pack living also has some disadvantages. There are more mouths to feed, which may prove to be a serious factor should there be a shortage in the food supply. In addition, in order to achieve the full benefits of cooperative hunting it is necessary to have a similar system of cooperative feeding. A

Siberian Huskies and Alaskan Malamutes are still used as sled dogs in the Northern wilds. Many of these dogs develop social hierarchies similar to those observed in wolf packs.

system of organization is necessary so that disputes may be settled quickly and efficiently in an attempt to promote harmony within the group and allow for the coordination of routine daily activities.

In 1935, Schelderup Ebbe discovered a *pecking order* in domestic chickens, in which each member has a particular social status and adopts a corresponding position on the social ladder with respect to all the other members. Thus, the highest ranking bird will peck all the other members of the flock without being pecked itself. The second highest bird will only tolerate pecking from the highest member yet will peck all the other birds. The same principle applies to the third, fourth, and fifth ranking birds and continues down the linear hierarchy.

A similar system of social organization has been described for wolves and is more commonly known as a *dominance hierarchy*. It has been suggested that the social hierarchy becomes established very early during puppyhood, at which time there appears to be a single rudimentary hierarchy. However, once male and female cubs reach adolescence, separate male and female hierarchies tend to develop. The highest ranking animals in each lineage are known as the alpha male and the alpha female. It is thought that pairs of wolves form complementary *dominant/subordinant relationships*, which altogether contribute to the dominance hierarchy of the entire pack. Rank is thought to be established during aggressive encounters, whereby one wolf dominates the other and in so doing establishes or confirms its superior position in the hierarchy. On the whole males are dominant to females, but this is not to say that all males are dominant to all females. On the contrary, the alpha and other high ranking females may be superior in rank to a large number of males.

This description, however oversimplified, provides useful guidelines for an insight into the basic principles underlying the social behavior of our good friend, *Canis familiaris,* the domestic dog.

SOCIAL SYSTEMS OF DOMESTIC DOGS

To a large extent, the generally accepted pattern of dog social behavior, with which most dog owners are familiar, has been based on knowledge about the social organization of wolves. Wolves and domestic dogs, although belonging to the same genus, experience very different environments. Wolves live in the wild, are social animals and normally run in packs, which form the basis of the social organization. In contrast, domestic dogs entertain a number of varied environments, depending on their particular station in life: whether as pet or working dog; whether it lives in the home or outside, in the country or city, with other dogs, animals or humans.

In the majority of instances, pack formation in domestic dogs would seem to be an exception rather than the rule. Even when rural, or more usually, urban dog packs are formed, the membership is quite fluid and the composition of the pack often changes from day to day. Moreover, domestic dogs are housed individually and the most common social interactions with other dogs are dyadic, that is to say on a one-to-one basis. Nevertheless, these dyadic interactions are similar to those occurring between wolves, and if a group of dogs has the opportunity to remain together for any length of time, they quickly establish stable hierarchies, comparable to those observed in a wolf pack.

To say that the hierarchy is the sole basis of dog social behavior would be incorrect. The notion of hierarchies has been much overplayed. For the most part, dogs seem to live in relative harmony with each member of the group, each generally going about its business with an apparent disinterest in the affairs of others. Having an established hierarchy really only comes into play during disputes, at times when dogs are competing for a valuable commodity which is in short or limited supply, such as when two dogs have their eyes on one bone, or in occasional instances where two males compete for a female in heat.

Rather than thinking in terms of a single hierarchy that determines the outcome of any and every interaction, it is important to consider the structure of the hierarchy in terms of the individual participants. The outcome of a dispute often depends on how valuable a dog considers the potential prize (how much dogs like

Often the nucleus of a social group is a litter that has had the opportunity to remain together. The pups grow up with adults, whose working social system serves as a model for the developing puppies.

85

A Beagle who has been chewing on an oxtail bone notices the approach of another dog.

The Beagle relinquishes possession of the bone without any resistance. The new possessor begins to "stare down" his adversary.

The new possessor carries the bone away to ensure its safety. Notice the position of his tail; arched over the back with a vibrating tip.

bones, for example). It is more accurate to think of a hierarchy in terms of individuals competing with each other. The result of the competition may depend not only on the established hierarchy but also upon the motivation of the individuals involved. Appreciation of the individuality of each group member is essential before one forms a realistic notion of social organization. It should be remembered that each dog has its own personality, or behavior profile. Each dog is different from all others, each interaction between any two dogs is different from all other interactions, and as such the structure of each group is unique. Moreover, the personalities of individual dogs, the interactions between them and the resulting group structures are ever changing in subtle and gradual ways.

Thus, in some ways the term "social organization" is misleading, since it conjures a permanent code of canine morés and laws to which all likely group members must adhere. Instead, it is the *group of individuals* that is unique in its flexible variability, as the group arrives at a workable system to promote an efficient and harmonious living situation. The organization that they adopt will vary from group to group depending on the individual membership and a wide variety of other variables. As such, it is more worthwhile and meaningful to approach an analysis on three different levels. First, and perhaps most important, from the viewpoint of the *individuals;* second, the *interactions* between these individuals; and third, the resulting system of apparent *social structure.*

Individuality

Although all dog owners are well aware that their dogs are individuals, this is a fact that many researchers in canine behavior tend to neglect or ignore completely. Breed variations and complex individual differences are often averaged out to arrive at a definition of a statistically typical textbook dog, which in reality does not exist. The theme of this book, *that a dog is a dog is a dog,* must not be overplayed. It is extremely important only when considering dogs as compared with other animals, but when considering dogs in their social context, individuality is a crucial factor. Dogs differ in the many factors that have been discussed in preceding chapters: size, shape, sensory abilities and mental capacities. Perhaps more importantly, behavioral development is different for each individual, depending on: parental genes, maternal behavior, early interactions with littermates, the owner and the home environment. The behavioral development of each individual is an intricate process. Some of the determining factors are directly observable, others are more subtle and indirect. If this were not sufficiently complicated, when considering social behavior, it is important to realize that the personality of each dog is constantly changing, depending on the environmental variables in adult life. One of the important considerations in this respect is interaction with other dogs.

Interactions

The traditional notion of interaction between dogs is one of a dyadic dominant/subordinate relationship. This is to say that when two dogs encounter each other, one dominates the other. This is a useful framework for an initial analysis, but again it is far too simple and rigid to fully explain a complex situation. In some cases, this concept of dominance and subordinance is actually misleading and does not accurately describe the functioning of the social system. Situations whereby a dog of higher rank physically dominates another individual are quite rare. For instance, in cases of dispute, such as two dogs and one bone, each individual will employ a variety of strategies in order to achieve and/or maintain possession of the bone.

Possession. If one dog is in possession of a bone at the start of an encounter, it has a distinct advantage, much like playing a home game. In the majority of cases, possession is nine tenths of canine law and many dogs may keep a bone from higher ranking individuals. In such cases, the behaviors that led to the finding of the bone are reinforced, thus *rewarding the initiative.* Only a very high ranking dog will dispute the ownership of a bone once it is in the possession of another. This may be achieved by confidently wandering over and assuming ownership, or by a lengthy process of wearing the opponent down by a series of bluffs and threats.

Confidence. In the face of a potential dispute, one dog may command the situation from the outset, although this need not be the so-called dominant individual. Strangely enough, in many cases, it

The dog who is in possession of a bone at the start of an encounter has a distinct advantage over the other dogs who may later approach. Possession appears to be nine tenths of canine law.

appears to be the dog of lower rank that is controlling the situation, even though it may be doing so by "opting out." In the majority of interactions between two dogs of established rank, the "underdog" will show no intention of attempting to seize the bone. On the contrary, it may start to walk nonchalantly in the opposite direction, seemingly unaware of the situation at hand. In cases where the subordinate animal already has possession of the bone, it will drop it and retreat immediately when a dog of higher rank approaches. Both dogs appear to be confident of the outcome; one dog is confident that it will win and the other is confident that it will lose.

Bluff. In encounters between dogs that are very similar in rank, or between dogs that are unfamiliar with each other, the resolution is often less clear-cut because both dogs are uncertain of the potential outcome. In such situations, it is not uncommon for the two dogs to try to stare each other down, continually threatening each other with growls, snarls and barks. The atmosphere seems very

Occasionally, a dispute between dogs may be settled by a fight. Such a fight might ensue if one dog oversteps its bounds, and ignores the warnings given by a dog of superior rank.

tense, as if at any moment the confrontation will erupt into the most horrendous dog fight. Instead, one dog eventually gives in and signals that it is declining the gambit and terminating the standoff by turning its head to one side. Characteristically, the loser will wander away and perhaps proceed to urinate with a nonchalance which might seem to suggest that the entire encounter was nothing but a bad dream.

Occasionally, disputes may be settled by a fight. A fight may ensue if one dog oversteps its bounds and ignores the warnings of another dog of established superior rank. This type of fight is usually extremely quick and takes the form of a brief attack with only a couple of snaps and bites from the higher-ranking dog. It is usually a one-sided affair, and the reprimanded animal may actively show signs of submission by rolling over on its back or making a hasty retreat. Sometimes the subordinate individual may start snapping defensively and fight back out of fear.

A very different type of fight may occur between two dogs of

90

similar rank when they are both unsure of the outcome. This is a terrible spectacle to watch and listen to. Both dogs continually growl, snarl and snap at each other and may square off on their hind legs as if they are boxing. Even so, serious bites during one-to-one dog fights are fairly infrequent.

Reinforcing the Initiative. Once a dispute has been settled, the behavior of the winner abruptly changes. Instead of the threatening insecure individual that was bluffing its way through the encounter, the dog now wallows in the confidence of its recent success and often assumes a picture of ultimate machismo. It proudly picks up the bone and with tail held high, swaggers off to some secluded corner to nibble on the prize. Some dogs will stare down the loser until it retreats a sufficient distance, whereupon the victor may pick up the bone and swagger past the defeated individual. Another type of this behavior may occur after a dispute has been settled by a fight. If the loser shows signs of submission, the victor may continue snapping and barking directly in front of the defeated dog. Such behaviors are convenient means of *reinforcing* the initiative. Once one dog has achieved an undisputed victory, it proceeds to advertise the fact to the defeated individual. Not only does this accentuate the victory and demoralize the underdog, but it may affect the outcome of subsequent encounters.

Frequently, a dog will advertise its authority by continually harassing a lower-ranking individual. Many of these encounters often seem unprovoked, and the higher-ranking dog will approach and growl until the other shows signs of appeasement. This usually occurs between members of the same sex, especially between male dogs of similar rank.

The result of one interaction has a substantial influence on, and is a good predictor of, what is likely to happen between the two dogs in the future. Similarly, the outcome may have indirect effects on the future associations with other dogs, such that winning an encounter with one dog might conceivably make the victor more confident in its relationship with other likely contestants.

Social Structure

If pairs of dogs have resolved their differences and can coexist peacefully, it is the first step toward having a large group of dogs

Above: A litter of puppies will usually feed peacefully from a food dish. However, in this example, the male tries to defend the entire dish, while his three sisters are busy eating. Below: Feeding times often precipitated a fight between the male and the highest ranking female.

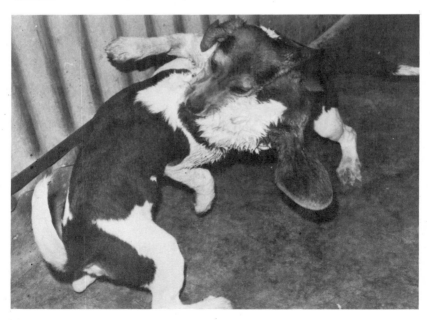

Fights between puppies are usually quite lengthy and are interspersed with periods of boxing, during which one dog will get hold of the other and wrestle it to the ground. Generally, the physical damage is minimal, and limited to small puncture wounds on the ears and scruff of the neck. The fight often ends when both pups are exhausted.

get along. Separate dyadic interactions between individual dogs form elementary building blocks for a system of social organization. From dyadic interactions, it is possible to infer a linear hierarchy useful as a framework in assessing the relative rank of a group of individuals. The male hierarchy is extremely stable, whereas the rank of individual females may vary slightly from week to week.

The social structure of domestic dogs is far more complex than that of dyadic relationships and the ensuing hierarchies. The presence of a third dog may further complicate matters. For example, when a bone was thrown out to two females, Joan and Doris, the first dog to get the bone was always Doris but then Joan would take it away from her immediately. However, if Ken were released, he would expropriate the bone from Joan and allow Doris to share. Examples like this are numerous and depend on the preferences, affiliations and personalities of the individuals concerned. Males will often share a bone with females but only on rare occasions will they share with other males, and similarly females will seldom share with females. Sometimes, the mere presence of one dog will influence the behavior of another.

The fact that the social structure of domestic dogs is not a rigid system cannot be over-emphasized. Instead, it is necessarily flexible and continually undergoes change. With domestic dogs, the membership of the social group may vary from day to day; similarly, a variety of external variables may have a significant influence. For instance, the area available to dogs, their feeding schedules at home, or the availability of food that may be scavenged may have a bearing on the degree and frequency of social interaction. Even within a domestic pack with a fairly stable membership, the role of individuals may change from day to day, which makes it imperative to view social organization in a developmental context.

Development of Social Structure. Often, the nucleus of a social group of feral dogs is a litter that has remained together. More often, the pups have grown up within a group of adults that have already established a working social system, which in itself serves as a model for the developing puppies.

A rudimentary hierarchy may be seen in a litter that is only one or two weeks old. At this stage, size and strength appear to be the

Adult dogs are surprisingly lenient with young pups, and will often allow a puppy to chew on a bone. However, the adults become much stricter as the pups grow older.

determining factors. The heavier pups are more likely to push other pups from a teat, rather than try and locate one for themselves. This is a self-reinforcing mechanism, whereby the larger pups establish primary access to their mother's milk, and by so doing they become even larger. After they have gorged themselves and are enjoying a postprandial nap, the smaller litter-mates then take their turn. However, within a few days, the smaller pups become opportunists and are quite adept at locating a vacant teat. Even at this early age, it is apparent that the litter is comprised of a group of individuals.

In most litters, by the time the pups are three or four weeks old, a top dog has firmly established its position, and an underdog is similarly apparent, whereas it may take several weeks before the middle order of the hierarchy becomes stabilized. Both the top dog and underdog quickly become certain of their position in the hierarchy, since they may both make generalizations about their social interactions. One is secure in the knowledge that it is superior in rank to all its littermates, whereas the underdog may make the assumption that it is universally inferior. For the remaining pups, the problem is more complicated, for they must learn to discriminate between dogs of higher and lower rank. To fail to recognize a lower ranking individual is usually of little importance, but if a puppy makes a mistake with a higher ranking dog it usually has to suffer the consequences.

Adult dogs will allow puppies a certain degree of playful license for the first few months of their life. Some adults are surprisingly tolerant toward the misbehavior of boisterous pups, whereas others employ avoidance tactics and growl if the pups come too close. As the pups grow older, the leniency of the adult dogs begins to wane. Male adults are much stricter than females with the pups, who quickly learn which adults they must respect and those which they may take liberties with. The male adults pay particular attention to the male pups, especially as the latter approach puberty. Periodically, the adults will intimidate pups by following them around. The young male pups also play their part in maintaining the harmony of the group by demonstrating active appeasement. They will take the initiative and with tails tucked between their legs, will approach higher ranking animals, which normally stand over the pups growling, while the younger dogs characteristically reach up to lick the muzzle of their social superior.

And of course, when the females reach puberty and come into heat, the social organization assumes a whole new enchilada.

5. Sexual Behavior

PUBERTY

Puberty marks the time when dogs attain sexual maturity and acquire the ability to mate and produce offspring. Puberty usually commences between six and nine months of age, although there is considerable breed and individual variation and the timing may differ greatly from breed to breed, usually occurring earlier in the smaller breeds. Similarly, environmental factors such as the time of year, food supply and the social situation would seem to have a profound influence. With females, the change from adolescence to adulthood occurs fairly abruptly and is clearly marked by the initial heat period, during which they will permit mating for the first time. However, with males, the transition is much more protracted.

In male dogs, the abdominal testes descend into the scrotum at a very early age. In fact, the majority of puppies are born with their testes descended. However, the scrotal testes do not begin to produce appreciable amounts of the male sex hormone, testosterone, until about twelve weeks of age, reaching a peak by seven to ten months. The rising levels of testosterone are responsible for the maturation of some secondary sexual characteristics in the male: an increase in the frequency of urination; the maintenance of accessory reproductive structures, such as the prostate gland; and the development of the full expression of adult mating behaviors.

A further change occurring at puberty in the male is the urination posture. Instead of employing the characteristic juvenile "stand-lean" posture, the male now commences to lift its hind leg. However, this change appears to be completely independent of the levels of male sex hormone, since even dogs castrated before puberty will start to use the adult male urination posture at about this time. Nevertheless, the increased levels of testosterone change the odor of the dog's urine so that it now smells like a male's, and other dogs are apt to treat it accordingly.

A bitch becomes very attractive to males during her estrous period, and they will come from blocks around in pursuit of her.

Once the male dog has reached puberty, it is normally fertile and able to mate all year round. Sperm have been recovered from the urine of dogs over sixteen years of age, indicating that they would, even at that advanced age, be able to impregnate a bitch provided that they had the inclination to mate (and most male dogs do). The bitch, on the other hand, is only receptive to a male for short "heat" (or estrous) periods during the year.

ESTROUS CYCLE

The bitch is *seasonally monestrous;* that is, she has only one heat period or *estrus* per season, and usually about two breeding seasons per year, although the frequency of seasons depends on the individual. Normally, a domestic bitch may come into heat at any time of the year, but there is evidence of seasonal occurrence of heat periods, as suggested by peak periods of conception during early spring and to a lesser extent in autumn. The estrous cycle of the bitch consists of four fairly distinct phases; *proestrus, estrus, metestrus* and *anestrus.*

Proestrus normally lasts for about nine days, although there may be considerable variation. Periods have been observed as long as three weeks and occasionally as short as one or two days. A reliable sign that a bitch is coming into season is the appearance of a bloody discharge* from her vulva, often first observed as conspicuous red drips on a kitchen floor or rug. The bitch spends more time sniffing and licking her vulva, which becomes more swollen and turgid as proestrus progresses. During this time, the females' urine and vaginal secretions become increasingly attractive to male dogs. The behavior of the bitch changes during proestrus. She becomes increasingly more active and restless and will walk for longer distances, wandering over a larger area. She shows signs of *polydipsia* and *polyuria* (increased frequeny of drinking and urination). She deposits trails of extremely attractive urine over a large area, and by the time she comes into estrus she is irresistibly centripetal to male dogs, who tend to converge at the bitch's place of residence. At this stage, males are extremely excited and often try to mount the female. During proestrus, the female will not stand for the male. When he attempts to mount, she will promptly sit down, or perhaps whirl around, prance and run away, usually with the male in hot pursuit. Some bitches will threaten a male, growling, biting, and chasing him away. As the female comes into heat, she shows much more interest in the male and the approach/retreat behavior is characteristic of this phase.

Estrus is the only time that a bitch is receptive toward a male's advances, and will allow mating to take place. The term is derived from the Latin *oestrus* and the Greek *oistros*, meaning "frenzy,"

---

*The sanguinous discharge in the estrous cycle of the bitch is often confused with the periodic hemorrhagic discharge that occurs during the menstrual cycle of primates. The menstrual changes refer to a periodic cycle desquamation of the uterine lining accompanied by a hemorrhagic discharge from arterioles and pools of extravasated blood. In contrast, the estrous hemorrhage in bitches is caused by diapedesis (oozing of blood through the walls of unruptured arterioles) in the vagina. The timing of the hemorrhage is also different. In the dog, the discharge occurs before ovulation as the vagina is being prepared for copulation, whereas in primates the menstrual discharge occurs after ovulation from breakdown of the uterine wall that had been prepared for the possible implantation of fertilized eggs.

Above: An estrous female is extremely attractive to male dogs. In this example she is pursued by two prospective suitors. Below: Some dogs will indulge in a lengthy sequence of courtship behaviors prior to mating. Here, the male prances alongside the female.

Much of the female's courtship behavior involves running towards the male and then retreating. This incites the male to give chase and ensures that he is oriented in the correct direction. Below: The female stops to enable the male to investigate her vulva.

which more than adequately explains the behavior of females and their male suitors during this phase. Estrus usually lasts for about nine days, and on the average, ovulation occurs spontaneously around the second day, whether the bitch has mated or not. (This is unlike cats, who are induced ovulators; ovulation occurs as a result of coital stimulation, after which the heat period will terminate within a couple of days). If a bitch is not mated, estrus may last as long as two to three weeks. During estrus, the vulva remains swollen and a drop of vaginal discharge may be seen at the tip of the vulva. With the progression of estrus, the coloration of the discharge may vary from bright red to brown. Occasionally, it may turn to a clear straw color, and eventually the discharge turns milky white towards the end of estrus. However, it is certainly false to assume that the heat period is over merely because the hemorrhagic discharge has ceased. The only certain way to determine whether the estrous phase has terminated is to test the bitch with a couple of males and see if she will stand and allow them to mount. (Unless you have quick reflexes, it is best to do this with a chastity belt fitted on the bitch).

Metestrus immediately follows estrus and lasts for a period of approximately two months.

If the bitch has been mated and fertilization has occurred, then metestrus is the period of pregnancy; if not, it is the period of pseudopregnancy.

Anestrus is the period of reproductive inactivity between seasons. The vulva is small and there is only a minimal vaginal discharge.

Control of the Estrous Cycle

At the base of the brain is a small area called the hypothalamus, which produces releasing factors that control the level of two gonadotrophic hormones, *follicle stimulating hormone* (FSH) and *luteinizing hormone* (LH) from the anterior pituitary gland. FSH stimulates the growth of ovarian follicles and sensitizes the ovary to LH, which triggers ovulation. The eggs leave the ruptured follicles and pass down the uterine tubes to await sperm that may be on the way up. The ovary produces two types of steroid hormones, which cause many of the physiological and behavioral changes during the estrous cycle. *Estrogen* is secreted from the growing follicles and is essential for behavioral receptivity at the time of ovulation. Estrogen is also responsible for vulval swelling, increased vaginal discharge, and the increase in attractiveness of estrous urine and vaginal secretions. *Progesterone* is secreted by the *corpora lutea,* which are formed from the remains of ruptured follicles following ovulation. Progesterone causes glandular growth of the uterus in preparation for the implantation of fertilized ova. High levels of progesterone are initially necessary for the maintenance of pregnancy.

A number of environmental conditions exert effects on the estrous cycle: the nutritional status of the animal, the temperature, the length of daylight and a variety of social factors. Puberty is delayed in bitches that have been fed a poor diet, and it has been suggested that feeding a bitch on a high nutritional plane, especially immediately prior to the heat period, increases the number of follicles that mature and ovulate. A modified diet is also advisable for heavily pregnant and lactating bitches. Similarly, in the male, deficient nutrition may cause a decrease in the volume of semen and the concentration of sperm. However, it has been suggested

Pursuit, by a male, of the bitch in estrus may prove frustrating to the bitch's owners, as the neighborhood will be besieged by numerous males, each intent on mating.

that starvation may actually increase the sperm count. It is certainly true that stud males will often neglect food when courting a bitch in heat, but in this situation, it is probably the excitement of courting rather than the temporary starvation that causes the increased sperm count. It is generally accepted that malnutrition causes decreased fertility and the dog should not be allowed to lose condition due to a shortage of calories. However, at the other extreme, it is true that an extremely obese animal is less inclined to mate.

The estrous cycle of a bitch appears to be affected by the amount of daylight, and bitches generally come into heat during periods of greater daylight, rather than in the winter months. There is thought to be a period of peak conception in the spring and perhaps a lesser peak in the autumn. These effects are less obvious in the male dog but it is probably true to say that they are keener on stud work in the spring. This may be because more bitches come into heat during those times, or simply that it is too cold in the winter and too hot in the summer.

It has been observed that in warmer climates, puberty occurs at an earlier age, and also that the anestrous periods between subsequent heats are shorter. However, excesses of temperature are often associated with failure of heats to occur. Quite often, the transportation of bitches from a temperate climate to the tropics causes a prolonged anestrus. The bitch will usually come into heat once she has become adapted to the new climatic conditions. However, for the most part, in the domestic environment, central heating and air conditioning tend to mask the effects of the climate.

MATING

Usually, mating presents no problems, provided the dog is keen and the bitch is at the appropriate stage of her estrous cycle. In the majority of cases, the mating seems to follow a specific canine choreography, a behavioral sequence that is unique and characteristic of dogs. The prospective mates approach, usually with speed, and then they proceed to investigate each other, first nose to nose, sniffing each other's muzzle, then side by side, investigating the other's anal and genital areas. The female's investigations tend to be more cursory than the male's, who usually spends considerable time sniffing and licking the vulva of an estrous bitch. The male often sniffs the tail and hocks of the female, which may be coated with vaginal secretions that have dripped from the vulva, and occasionally the male may sniff or lick the female's ears.

The male usually rests his chin over the female's back, whereupon he mounts her from the rear, and with his forelegs he clasps the females around the flanks immediately anterior to the hip joints. Once mounted, the male executes a series of pelvic thrusts which tend to direct his penis in the general direction of the vulval aperture. It may take several mounts to achieve the correct orientation, whereupon the insertion thrust is quite obvious and the male will flatten his pelvic region against the female, depress his tail and clasp her tightly with his forelegs. The insertion thrust is followed by a unique "behavior of intromission," whereby the male exhibits a series of pelvic oscillations and rapid thrusting and displays treading movements with his hind legs. During this behavior the prepuce is pushed back beyond the bulb of the gland and full erection of the penis takes place. The bulb of the penis becomes considerably enlarged and is held inside the bitch by the constrictor muscles of the vagina. This holds the male in position until ejaculation is completed and constitutes the so-called "tie" or "lock" service. The male will usually drop his forelegs to one side and then after a short time he will lift one hindleg over the back of the female so that the copulating couple are standing rear to rear, facing away from each other with the male's penis reflected backward between his legs. In this position, the lock usually lasts for about 25 minutes, although the duration may be as short as five minutes or as long as an hour and a quarter.

The reason for this strange position is obscure. It has been suggested that this behavior has been retained from the wild, where the mating couple would be vulnerable to attack; so, they engineered a position that sports teeth at both ends. Another suggestion is that the lock is a more comfortable position for the male, although this is extremely difficult to imagine. It was initially thought that the prolonged vaginal and cervical stimulation during the lock was necessary for a fertile mating. However, in some individuals and particularly some breeds, such as Chows, a tie

Above: The male mounts the female from the rear. Notice that her tail is deviated to one side. Below: During the insertion thrust, the male depresses his tail and executes a series of rapid thrusts as intromission is achieved.

Above: After several minutes, the couple is "locked" together, the male dismounts, and they stand rear to rear or alongside each other. Below: The "lock" normally lasts for about half an hour.

rarely occurs during mating, and yet their breeding records are good. The ejaculation of the sperm-bearing fraction of semen occurs shortly after insertion and it would appear that a tie is not necessary for fertilization. However, the subsequent ejaculation of the large volume of prostatic semen serves to wash in and activate the sperm, thus maximizing the probability of a fertile mating. In this respect, the reflection of the penis through the hind legs may aid this process by increasing the pressure of the ejaculate.

Although the function of the lock still remains somewhat obscure, the reason how it comes about is better understood. Vaginal stimulation at the root of the penis stimulates the complete erection of the *bulbus glandis* as it becomes engorged with blood. Constriction of the vulval musculature behind the tumescent bulb prevents its removal from the vagina. However, in the same way that the erect *bulbus glandis* prevents the penis from leaving the vagina, it is similarly impossible for a fully erect penis to achieve intromission. If perchance the penis slips out while full erection is taking place, the bitch becomes extremely excited and is apt to prance and whirl about the male, quite often mounting him. Occasionally, she will lick the tip of his penis, and stimulation of this area causes reflex detumescence of the *bulbus glandis,* which makes subsequent penetration possible.

Generally, the pattern of mating behavior of all domestic dogs follows the same basic sequence as outlined above, but the speed and duration of the various phases is extremely variable and depends on the experience and temperament of both partners. Prospective mates appear to show more variation during courtship and the appetitive stages of mating. As the consumatory phase is neared, the pattern of behaviors more closely resembles a stereotyped sequence that is characteristic of all *Canidae.*

Depending on their age, sexual experience and general disposition, male dogs will show wide variation in their courtship activities, and the resilience of some males is commendable at the least, and incredulous at the most. Prospective suitors employ a wide range of ploys to determine the estrous state of females. One male may spend considerable time playing with the female and chasing her, and perform a prolonged investigation of her muzzle, ears, body and tail, especially sniffing and licking the vulva, before

Stimulated by the male's lack of enthusiasm, the female prances and paws at his brisket.

The male fails to respond and so the female puts her paws on his back.

Here, the bitch finally attempts to mount the male.

actually attempting to mount. Another male may simply rush in and mount almost anything that moves, obviously unaware of the canine olfactory pleasantries designed to tell him whether the mountee is male or female, or whether the female is in heat or not. Instead, he relies on the response to his mount, to see if he has indeed chosen a bitch in heat.

Male dogs normally have little difficulty in demonstrating their ability to mount and thrust, but some, especially young or naive dogs, have difficulty in assuming the correct orientation and can often be seen mounting the front end or the side of a female. In the heat of the moment, even an experienced stud may occasionally mount the head of an otherwise receptive female. Even once they have assumed the characteristic posture, some males have difficulty in making the finer adjustments and will simply thrust away frantically in the general direction of the female's rear. It is common for some males to mount several times before achieving intromission. Other individuals may spend more time inspecting the precise location of the vulva, after which pelvic thrusting is a more refined and delicate affair, and it is not uncommon for intromission to be achieved almost immediately on the first mount.

Many people are under the assumption that the male plays the major role in mating, and the female is often viewed not even as a co-star, but as an extra. This, of course, is completely erroneous. The function of mating is to engineer spermatozoa and ova into close proximity so as to maximize the probability that fertilization will take place. In order to meet this end, the essential problem is to maneuver the penis into the vagina, and the female certainly plays an equal and active role in this endeavor. At the height of estrus, a female is just as eager to get to a male as he is to her. Much of her classic soliciting behavior involves first running towards the male and then away from him. If the male does not follow, the bitch will approach once more, prance around, strike his body with her forepaws and even mount him to arouse his attention, only to run away again. The "teasing" behavior of the female generally incites the male to chase her, usually with his nose only an inch or two from her rear. At this point, the male is oriented in the correct direction. Some males will follow slightly to one side with their chin over the back of the female, and when she stops, will mount her immediately. Should the male still get it wrong and attempt to mount the female's head or side, she will pull away, whirl around and run off once more. In the height of estrus, seasoned bitches will prominently present their hindquarters to the male's nose, whereupon she will characteristically deviate her tail to one side, thus exposing her vulva. When considering mating behavior, the bitch's contribution should not be viewed in terms of the passivity of a mere recepticle. Instead, the bitch's receptivity bears close resemblance to that of a wide receiver in football, in which the quarterback lobs the ball in a general forward direction, but it is the expertise and manueverability of the receiver that makes sure the pass is completed.

Once mounted in the correct fashion, many of the fine postural adjustments that are necessary for intromission are in fact executed by the bitch. If the male's thrusting is too high, she will tip her vulva upwards, and if he is too low, she will flex her hind legs.

The bitch performs many of the fine postural adjustments necessary for intromission. Notice that her tail is deviated to one side.

Similarly, if he is thrusting too far to one side, she will deviate her flanks laterally to compensate for the discrepancy. Alternatively, she will sweep her tail to one side, brushing the penis in the intended direction.

The female's behavior continually changes from day to day throughout the estrous cycle. She will start to seek out males as soon as she comes into proestrus, at which time male dogs begin to find her increasingly attractive. Similarly, the bitch's receptivity waxes and wanes throughout estrus, generally reaching a peak around the fourth day (about two days after ovulation, when the ova are ready for fertilization). Different degrees of receptivity are often attributed to variations in the female's overall level of sexual responsiveness, which would affect her behavior toward all males. This is the case with promiscuous females, who will mate with any male that happens to come along. However, some bitches will mate readily with certain male partners, and actively resist the courtship and mating attempts of others. Female mating preferences appear to be comparatively stable over several breeding seasons and may last for many years. The preference patterns vary substantially between females, but it is not unusual for some stud males to be universally popular or unpopular. It is not known exactly which male qualities the females find attractive or displeasing, but these preferences are probably influenced by the mating ability of the male. It seems that a bitch will much rather accept an efficient copulator rather than a slow, clumsy, bumbling male.

Anestrous bitches also exhibit varying degrees of social affinity for different males with whom they have been reared. However, under the influence of the hormonal conditions associated with estrus, these social preferences become overridden by an entirely different pattern of sexual preferences, which do not appear to have any relationship with previous social preferences or the hierarchical structure of the social group. There is some evidence to suggest that male dogs have similar mating preferences, but they appear to be magnifications of existing social preferences. More often than not, male dogs tend to be quite indiscriminate about their choice of mating partners and will eagerly mate with any female that is in estrus.

Why are females more selective than male dogs when choosing a potential mating partner? Males have the ability to mate and are fertile all the year 'round, whereas a bitch only comes into season twice a year. Once the female has mated, she will be pregnant for nine weeks; afterwards, she will supply the majority of food requirements of the litter for an additional two months or so until weaning is completed. For these reasons it is advantageous for bitches to be more particular with whom they mate, in an attempt to choose a complementary partner, with the view to produce a qualitatively viable litter. Once a female accepts a male as a mate, she has invested her time (half the breeding year) and energy for the care and feeding of her potential offspring. Male dogs invest comparatively little; a day's supply of sperm and a couple of hours at the most. If the male has made a bad choice he can attempt to mate with as many other females as possible. His insurance is quantity, hers is quality.

When testing a bitch to determine the appropriate time for mating, it is advisable to use more than one male. This minimizes the risk that the female is not refusing to "stand" simply because she does not like the suitor that has been chosen for her. The bitch may be fitted with a chastity belt and taken for a walk in the park. By testing the bitch during proestrus, it is possible to influence the sex ratio of pups in the litter. Normally, the bitch is mated on the second and fourth day and the resulting litter usually consists of an equal number of males and females. If a greater percentage of females is desired, the bitch should be mated on the first and second day, whereas if male pups are desired, the mating should be delayed until the fourth and fifth days.

ARTIFICIAL INSEMINATION

Artificial insemination involves the collection of semen from a stud male, and its subsequent introduction into the vagina of an estrous bitch, usually by means of a long pipette and syringe. The first documented case of a bitch producing live offspring following insemination with frozen canine semen occurred as early as 1696, and by the end of the eighteenth century Abbé Spallanzani was conducting research into methods of artificial insemination. Since then, the practice of artificial insemination in dogs has largely been on the experimental scale. In 1955, a litter of puppies was born at the Canine Research Centre at Newmarket, Great Britain,

A Beagle bitch photographed with litter whelped at Cornell University, Ithaca, New York. The bitch had been inseminated with semen 140
hours old, flown over from Great Britain. From *Reproduction in the
Dog,* by A. E. Harrop, pub. by Balliere, Tindall and Cox.

from semen that was 60 hours old and had been transported from
London by train and car. In 1956, a beagle bitch was inseminated
at Cornell University, Ithaca, New York, by semen that was 140
hours old and had been flown in from Great Britain. This was
probably a first in canine transatlantic artificial insemination.
Only within the last 20 years or so have better methods of diluting
and preserving semen come to light and it seems that now the
technique is becoming increasingly popular in breeding kennels.

The first and most obvious question is, why not let the dogs do
it themselves? Artificial insemination is quicker and less
troublesome, but also has several other important advantages over
a natural mating. It is extremely useful when a natural mating is
impossible due to the geographical distance between the bitch and
prospective stud. The female may be settled in Sewickley, Penn-
sylvania, whereas the stud may herald from Purfleet, Essex.
Moreover, it is sometimes impossible to transport the dog between
countries due to import or quarantine regulations. With some
animals, it is simply inadvisable to transport them over long
distances and it is considerably cheaper and less troublesome to
send a small vial of semen. Perhaps more important, the flexibility
afforded by artificial insemination may offset some of the unwanted side-effects of intensive selective breeding.

Artificial insemination may be employed when a natural mating
is impossible due to some behavioral or anatomical reason. A bitch

may refuse to mate with some males due to mating preferences discussed earlier. She may entirely disagree with the owner's choice of a prospective stud and instead prefer the local mongrel, which of course, is not conducive to breed conformation. Artificial insemination is useful when an expensive stud is unable to mate due to some anatomical abnormality, such as a broken hind leg. (It would *never* be used with dogs with abnormalities that have some hereditary disposition, such as lameness due to hip dysplasia).

Artificial insemination also serves to increase and extend the potential of a valuable stud. Sufficient semen may be collected, diluted and preserved to inseminate considerably more bitches than the dog could manage in its lifetime. The semen may be used long after the stud has passed away.

Artificial insemination is also a convenient means of disease prevention. The stud male is a focal point for the transmission of venereal diseases. The stud may be infected by any one of the large number of bitches that he comes in contact with, and once infected, if suitable precautions are not taken, the dog will infect practically every female that he serves. Prior to the collection of semen, the donor may undergo a physical examination to ensure

An artificial vagina devised by A. E. Harrop is one of three methods of semen collection for use in inseminating a bitch. From *Reproduction in the Dog.*

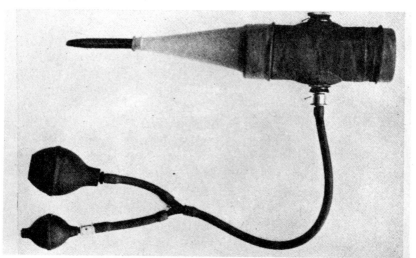

that he is free of any contagious disease. Once collected, the semen may be preserved with small amounts of an antibiotic, which will prevent the multiplication of any bacteria.

Methods of Semen Collection

There are three methods that have been used for collecting canine semen: digital manipulation, electrical stimulation and the use of an artificial vagina. Digital manipulation is more usually objected to on esthetic grounds, rather than by the qualitative and quantitative insufficiency of the semen obtained. An alternative method is to place electrodes in the rectum, and a short electric charge causes the dog to ejaculate. This method is not always reliable and quite often the semen is contaminated with urine. Also, a general anesthetic is usually necessary, which is an added disadvantage. Nowadays, the generally accepted method of collecting semen from a stud is by the use of an artificial vagina. Perhaps the most famous is Harrop's Canine Artificial Vagina. This consists of an outer rubber casing with a latex liner and the space in between these is filled with warm water, which may be pulsated by an attached rubber bladder. This particular artificial vagina has been extremely successful and may be adapted to any size dog. It is sold by Arnold and Sons, Wigmore Street, London.

The dog's ejaculate originates from three different sources. The ejaculation of the first fraction usually takes between 30-50 seconds and the volume may vary between 0.25 to 5 ml. Larger quantities may be collected if the stud has been stimulated by a bitch in estrus. The secretion contains no spermatozoa and is a clear watery fluid, which probably originates from the urethral glands of Littré. The second fraction is white and viscous. This is the testicular sperm-bearing fraction. The volume may vary from 0.5 to 3.5 ml and is ejaculated within 50-90 seconds. The third fraction is a clear watery prostatic secretion, which contains no spermatozoa. This fraction may vary considerably in volume, anywhere from 2 to 30 ml and is ejaculated within 5-35 minutes. The semen is normally fractionated upon collection by quickly changing the tubes between each fraction. (In a natural mating, the sperm-bearing fraction is normally ejaculated within the first couple of minutes following intromission and the large volume of prostatic fluid is ejaculated throughout the duration of the lock).

The volume of the semen may vary greatly between individuals and from one breed to another, with as little as 5 ml from a Beagle but up to 25 ml from a Greyhound. The sperm concentration may range from 4 to 588 million sperm per ml of semen, again depending on the breed and individual. Moreover, values varying from 4 to 540 million sperm per ml have been collected from the same dog on different occasions. (Both the frequency of previous ejaculations and inconsistencies in the collection of sperm-bearing and sperm-free fractions may cause substantial variations between samples.) When considering all breeds, the average volume of semen from a complete ejaculate is approximately 10 mls and the average concentration about 125 million spermatozoon per ml. This works out to be around 1 billion, 250 million spermatozoon per ejaculate to produce a few puppies.

The semen may be frozen in pellets, glass vials or straws. The most suitable dilutant is a mixture of egg yolk, glycerol, and lactose, which helps to protect the sperm against the freezing procedure, which involves temperatures as low as 320°F below zero. The sperm is thawed rapidly by immersion in water at the bitch's body temperature and it is ready for immediate use.

PREGNANCY

During ovulation, the ova are released from the rupturing ovarian follicles and pass slowly down the uterine tube, where they meet with spermatozoa and fertilization takes place. It has been shown that spermatozoa move quickly and may reach the site of fertilization within 25 seconds after ejaculation. The transport of sperm is probably greatly facilitated by antiperistaltic uterine waves. Ova may remain viable for about 12 hours and sperm for anytime up to four days. The fertilized ova become attached to the uterine wall by the formation of a placenta, through which nutrients and metabolites are transferred between mother and fetus. Ova are usually released from each ovary and they may migrate from one horn to the other, so that there is an even distribution between both uterine horns. On the average, pregnancy lasts for about 63 days, but again, there may be considerable individual and breed variations, and durations from 53 to 71 days may be quite normal.

Pseudopregnancy

If the bitch is not mated during estrus, she passes into the metestrus phase of her estrous cycle. Normally, this lasts for a little over two months, approximately the same duration as pregnancy. The hormonal changes that occur during metestrus are quite similar to those of pregnancy. In fact, in many bitches the hormonal changes during metestrus produce changes in physiology and behavior that would normally be typical of pregnancy. There may be a variable degree of uterine growth and the bitch may put on weight. The mammary glands may become considerably enlarged and even come into full milk after a couple of months. Many bitches become restless and may show a "phantom whelping," involving contractions of abdominal muscles and other behavioral changes almost identical to a normal parturition.

Pseudopregnancy in the bitch is a normal endocrinological event, representing a variable phsyiological and behavioral manifestation of the hormonal changes that occur during metestrus. Although the hormonal changes following estrus occur in all bitches, whether pregnant or not, it is unclear why there is a variation in the intensity of overt behavioral and physiological signs in non-pregnant individuals.

Many of the behavioral signs may be treated with sedatives and the mammary gland development may be suppressed by injections of testosterone. The bitch is treated primarily because both she and the owner often seem distressed by the behavioral disturbance. It is thought that pseudopregnancy may be associated with a higher incidence of pyometra, an accumulation of pus in the uterine cavity, caused by uterine infection.

Pregnancy Diagnosis

Pregnancy is the commonest cause of anestrus in animals (just as it is the commonest cause of amenorrhea in humans). This may be a useful sign in polyestrous females that have successive cycles throughout the year. However, it is not of much use in the bitch, which is seasonally monestrous, and has long anestrous periods between subsequent cycles. As discussed earlier, even in the absence of a fertile mating, each heat is followed by a period of metestrus or pseudopregnancy. The clinical manifestation of pseudopregnancy may closely resemble the signs of a normal pregnancy, which sometimes makes pregnancy diagnosis extremely difficult.

One of the cardinal signs of pregnancy is an increase in body weight resulting from the deposits of subcutaneous and abdominal fat. This becomes more apparent about the fifth week of pregnancy, when the abdomen may also appear to be slightly distended. However, this may not be altogether obvious in a bitch with only one or two fetuses. The gravid uterus does not cause much of an increase in body weight during the first month of pregnancy, but subsequent to this, the increase may be quite marked, varying from 2 pounds in a small bitch up to 16 pounds in a large bitch. By weighing the bitch at regular intervals before and after mating, and plotting the increases in weight, it should be possible to detect a growth curve characteristic of pregnancy.

The condition of the mammary glands also offers some indication of the reproductive state of the bitch. In bitches that are carrying their first litter, the changes are most apparent. At about the 35th day, the teats become enlarged and swollen and the unpigmented skin turns pink. As pregnancy progresses, the teats continue to enlarge but the turgidity decreases and they become much softer. By about the 50th day, there is usually an obvious amount of mammary growth. Milk may be expressed from the teats for a couple of days before parturition.

It is difficult to differentiate between pregnancy and pseudopregnancy on the basis of body weight, abdominal distension and mammary growth alone. The most reliable method of pregnancy diagnosis in the bitch is abdominal palpation. However, this should only be performed by a veterinary surgeon or an experienced breeder. If fetuses can be felt in the uterus, it is a certainty that the bitch is pregnant. There are several factors which determine the ease with which this may be carried out. The amount of abdominal fat and the temperament of the bitch are both important. A nervous bitch will often tense her abdominal muscles and make palpation extremely difficult. The period of pregnancy during which the examination is made and the number of fetuses are also important factors. If there are only one or two fetuses, they may be carried well forward and higher in the abdominal cavity, making them harder to detect. The optimal time for pregnancy diagnosis by abdominal palpation is between the 24th and 30th days. It is sometimes possible to palpate embryos as early as three weeks, at which time they are about an inch in diameter. If the bitch is small and not very fat, it may be possible to count the number of embryos. Later, an accurate diagnosis becomes more difficult. Although the uterus is in close apposition to the abdominal wall, the constricted portions of the uterus between embryos have become dilated so that the uterine horns are of uniform diameter. However, at six to seven weeks, the fetuses may be felt in the posterior part of the abdomen. This procedure may be facilitated by raising the forequarters of the bitch.

Pregnancy may also be detected by radiography and auscultation. By the end of the third week of pregnancy a vague uterine shadow may be evident upon X-ray. Positive diagnosis by X-ray is relatively easy after the seventh week, when the fetal vertebrae and rib cages may be reliably detected and counted. The main advantage of radiography lies in the ability to confirm pregnancy when only a single fetus is present and palpation is virtually impossible. In the last week, auscultation of the bitch's abdomen with a stethoscope will reveal fetal heartbeats.

Although biological tests for hormones in the blood or urine are useful in detecting pregnancy in humans and many domestic animals, they have not proved to be successful in bitches; the hormonal changes occuring during pregnancy are similar to those in metestrus.

WHELPING

If it is required that the bitch whelps in a special room, it is advisable that she be moved there at least several weeks beforehand, so that she may have adequate time to adjust to the new environment. The whelping box should be warm and preferably placed in a quiet, secluded area with sufficient ventilation. It is better to raise the box off the floor a few inches to prevent excessive drafts. Clean newspaper is suitable for bedding; it is sufficiently warm and may be frequently changed without much trouble or expense. General hygiene is important around the time of parturition, and an attempt should be made to keep the bitch in a clean, comfortable environment. It is important not to overfeed the bitch during the last few days of pregnancy. A *mild* laxative diet may also be advisable to prevent constipation, which might otherwise cause unnecessary straining and discomfort.

The behavior of the bitch changes toward the end of gestation. She is generally more restless and appears uncomfortable. She may show nesting behavior and start to tear up newspapers and to scratch at the floor of the whelping box. Often the bitch will go off her food, and some occasionally vomit during the few days immediately prior to parturition. It is not unusual for the bitch to pant a great deal and to regularly look apprehensively at her hindquarters.

The vulva will appear swollen, and a slight discharge of mucus may be present. At this stage, the mammary glands are considerably swollen and the onset of lactation is imminent. There is a relaxation of the *sacro-sciatic* and *sacro-iliac* ligaments, so that the hindquarters of the bitch appear to be low-slung, as if she has a lowered rear suspension. This allows the pelvis to rotate slightly, straightening the birth canal. There is also some degree of relaxation of the pubic symphysis, which increases the diameter of the birth canal.

As parturition commences, the involuntary muscular contractions of the uterus can be noticed at increasingly regular intervals. The bitch will usually lie down, occasionally licking her vulva and hindquarters between the periods of contraction.

In pregnancy, the spontaneous contractions of the uterus are inhibited by high levels of progesterone. Initially, progesterone is produced by the ovaries, and in the later stages of pregnancy by the fetal placentae. Toward the end of pregnancy, the local inhibition of placental progesterone decreases, and the spontaneous contractions of the uterus increase in strength and become more coordinated. It is thought that this is facilitated by rising levels of estrogen, which increase the excitability of the uterine muscle. As parturition proceeds and the head of the first puppy comes into contact with the cervix, the cervical stimulation initiates reflexive release of oxytocin hormone from the posterior pituitary gland at the base of the brain. Oxytocin acts on the estrogen-sensitized uterus and causes rhythmic peristaltic contractions.

Once the coordinated uterine contractions begin to increase in strength and frequency, the bitch may also show voluntary abdominal muscular contractions and very shortly the fetal mem-

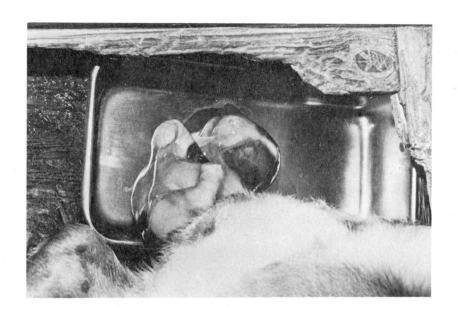

The newborn pup is enclosed in fetal membranes. Below: The fetal membranes of another pup protrude from the vulval aperture.

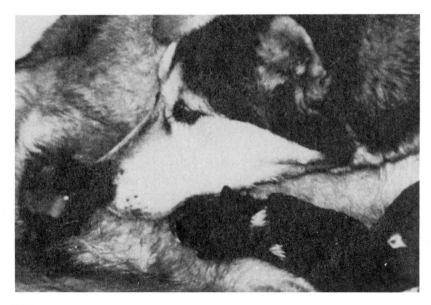

The bitch finds the fetal fluids extremely attractive and she proceeds to lick the newborn pup. Below: The bitch uses her incisors to bite through the fetal membranes.

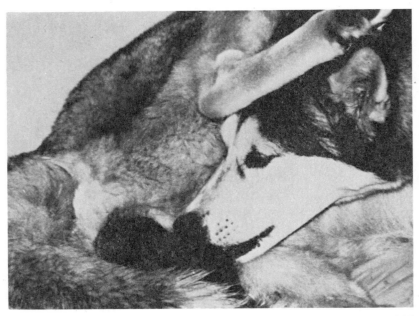

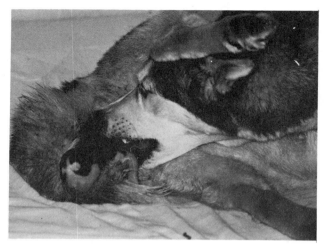

The bitch will assist in the birth process, tearing at the membranes that surround the pup and severing the umbilical cord with her teeth.

branes of the first puppy appear between the lips of the vulva. The fluid-filled membrane usually bursts under the pressure of straining. Otherwise, the bitch will rupture it by prolonged bouts of licking and chewing. The majority of bitches will lie down when giving birth, but there are those who whelp while sitting or standing.

The emergence of the head, which is the widest part of the puppy, takes the longest time, and then the rest of the body usually follows fairly easily. From the onset of straining, the birth of the first pup may take any time from a few minutes to an hour and a half. The puppy is completely enclosed in fetal membranes, and the umbilical cord is still intact. The bitch will tear at the membranes and sever the umbilical cord with her teeth and then vigorously lick the puppy. The licking stimulates the puppy's breathing, and within a few minutes it will show some activity and soon make its way to a vacant nipple and commence suckling. The rest of the fetal membranes and the placenta are generally voided shortly following the birth of the pup.

The onset of the next period of straining usually occurs within about half an hour. Less effort is required, and the birth of subsequent pups usually takes less time. Suckling stimulates the release of more oxytocin, which initiates the letdown of milk and facilitates further uterine contractions. Some bitches deliver puppies at regular intervals and will take only a short rest between

124

births. Others might have a long rest after the first puppy and then deliver several within a short period of time. Often there is a long pause between the last few puppies, especially if it is a large litter and the bitch is tired. A normal whelping may take anything from two to eight hours. It is usually a more experienced dam who whelps in a shorter period of time and with more regularity than a *primigravida*.

Help from the owner

If there are no signs of a puppy or fetal membranes within about three hours after the onset of true labor, it is generally assumed that complications have arisen and that expert assistance should be sought. It is recommended that the owner seek help *promptly*. With the removal of the obstructing fetus, the birth of subsequent

A Beagle bitch in the process of severing the umbilical cord of one of her newborn pups. Generally a bitch will know what to do as labor approaches and the birth process begins, but the owner should be nearby should complications arise.

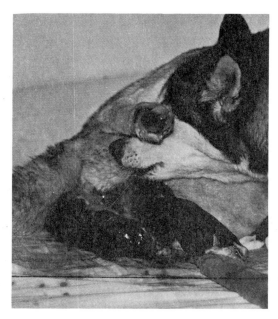

The bitch begins to chew through the umbilical cord. Below: After the fetal membranes have been removed, the bitch licks the pup. Stimulation to the umbilical area initiates respiration and the pup takes its first breath.

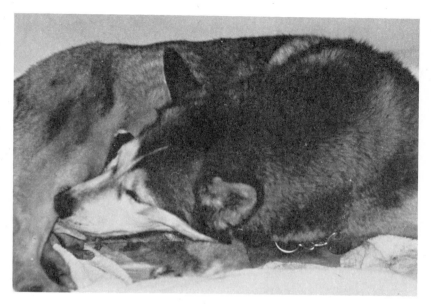

Above: Once the pup has been licked dry and has started to breathe, the dam licks the pup's anogenital area to stimulate urination and defecation. Below: The bitch goes through the same sequence of behaviors with each successive pup.

Above: The bitch will take periodic rests between pups. Below: The bitch enjoys a well earned sleep after the delivery of seven healthy Siberian Husky pups.

Above: The majority of dams will share food with their offspring, usually giving the pups prime access to it. Below: Some mothers will not permit the pups to eat her food. Instead, she will usually regurgitate semi-digested food.

puppies might follow without assistance. If the bitch is left to strain for too long, she might be too exhausted to continue whelping after corrective assistance.

Usually, it is best not to interfere with whelping, as some bitches actively resent any form of intrusion. Owner participation should be restricted to occasional inspections to make sure that all is well. Sometimes, however, the presence of the owner is a source of great comfort to a nervous and excitable bitch, especially if this is her first litter. The owner may help to clean and dry the puppies, particularly if the bitch appears disinterested. It may also be necessary to have to sever the umbilical cord. This can easily be done by tying off the cord with a piece of silk and cutting it with a clean pair of scissors about an inch from the puppy's abdomen. Occasionally, a little help is advantageous in the delivery of an extra large puppy. If the pup becomes stuck halfway out of the vulva, it may be grasped with a towel and gently but firmly pulled outward and downward. It is best to coordinate this manipulation with the uterine contractions and abdominal straining.

It is often asked whether it is advisable for the bitch to consume the afterbirths. They may cause a very mild gastric upset, but the major objection appears to be that this habit is esthetically displeasing to the owner. In the wild, a bitch would normally devour the afterbirths very soon after they are voided and they certainly provide an extremely nutritive food source. Also, it is a convenient way of disposing of evidence that a birth has taken place, which may help to protect the litter and bitch from potential predators. However, with the present day overfed and overprotected domestic dog, both of these functions have lost their adaptive value and consumption of the afterbirths does not appear to be essential for the health of the bitch. It seems that the dilemma can reasonably be left either to the inclination of the bitch or the whim of the owner.

MATERNAL BEHAVIOR

The mother finds the amniotic fluid extremely attractive and will actively sniff and lick the new pups as they arrive. This stimulates respiration and initiates immediate rooting behavior on behalf of the pups, which will begin to suckle as soon as they contact a teat. If the bitch is lying on her side with her limbs extended, her abdomen and fore and hind limbs form three sides of a rhomboid, which helps to funnel the pups toward the teats. If the pup is oriented in the wrong direction and is crawling away from the bitch, she will reach forward and bring it closer. For the first week, the bitch will retrieve any puppies that are removed from the nesting box. The pups are normally carried with the whole body in her mouth and the legs dangling downward. After one week, the pups become too large for the mother to pick up in this fashion and at this stage it is characteristic for the mother to push the pups along the ground with her open mouth. This appears to be quite efficient on a smooth floor but on rough terrain the pups invariably get plowed under.

During the first two weeks, the mother spends most of her time with the pups, only occasionally getting up to eat or relieve herself. Periodically, she will lick the pups, who will wake up and begin feeding. The bitch will lick the anus and genital areas of each pup, causing them to urinate and defecate. The bitch normally consumes their urine and feces. When the pups are two to three weeks old and are more active, the bitch will leave them for longer periods. The pups will sleep or play among themselves, and when the mother returns they run to greet her and immediately begin to suckle. By the time the pups are three to four weeks of age, they will readily consume their mother's feces, a convenient source of semi-solid nourishment. The majority of mothers will readily share their own food, usually giving the pups prime access. At this stage, solid food should be made available to the pups. Some bitches will regurgitate food in response to the pups' licking and sniffing her muzzle.

The mother will start the weaning process quite early. When the pups approach to suckle, she will stand up so that the teats are out of reach. After a couple of weeks, this ploy fails to work, since the puppies have grown enough to reach up to the teats. Instead, she may run away or growl when the pups attempt to suckle. Adult male domestic dogs rarely show any interest in the pups, which contrasts with male wolves, who have been observed vomiting food for the cubs.

Most dogs can be taught a remarkable number of commands fairly easily. At one level are the essential commands, such as "sit" and "come here." At another level are recreational commands, such as "beg" and "roll over" and at the highest level of performance are the obedience trials.

6. Training

Some dog owners question the necessity of training their pets, and instead would rather let their dogs run freely to determine how they want to conduct their own lives. This is unwise. There are two primary reasons why training should be obligatory. First, it is essential that a dog may be easily controlled if it is allowed to be in a public place, both for its own safety and to prevent it from becoming a nuisance. Dogs that kill chickens, chase sheep and roam crowded streets have extremely short life expectancies. Second, the owner quite often represents the dog's closest and most intimate companion, and in some cases the *only* companion. It is extremely difficult, (at least impractical) for humans to communicate with their dogs in canine fashion, but it is relatively easy to teach a dog the meaning of a wide variety of human words. Training greatly facilitates the working of the relationship between dog and human. It alleviates boredom and is undoubtedly enjoyable for the dog, as well as its owner.

Dog training involves some very simple conditioning techniques, a little patience and a great deal of common sense. This chapter is a brief review of the various types of conditioning procedures with greater emphasis on those experimental techniques which have an important bearing on the practical side of dog training. A good understanding of some of these elementary concepts will save much time and energy when the time comes to put theory to practice. Since there are a bevy of books available on the various schools of dog training, only a relatively simple and effective training schedule has been outlined here. For those who require a more detailed account, the most useful books are *Underdog* by Mordecai Siegel and Mathew Margolis, and *Dog Psychology: The Basis of Dog Training* by Leon Whitney.

Conditioning is the process whereby a dog may be trained to perform various tasks upon command, with the prospect of a suitable reinforcement. It is generally accepted that there are two types of conditioning: *classical conditioning* and *operant conditioning*.

Classical Conditioning

Classical conditioning is popularly synonymous with the Nobel prize-winning Russian scientist Ivan Petrovich Pavlov. His school was active at the beginning of this century and had a considerable influence on Russian behavioral studies. Pavlov's theories had less impact in the West, largely because of similar work by Sherrington, who studied the organization of spinal reflexes in dogs. Pavlov was primarily a physiologist, and his intention was to study "higher nervous activity." He also worked with dogs, and assumed that just as spinal reflexes were a property of the spinal cord, conditioned reflexes were a property of higher nervous centers. Palvov's experiments involved the salivatory reflex in dogs, whereby the taste of food stimulates salivation. In the process of classical conditioning, a completely new stimulus, which formerly had no effect on the unconditioning salivatory reflex, gains the power to elicit the respondent behavior (salivation). If the neutral stimulus is associated with the unconditioned stimulus for an adequate number of presentations, the previously neutral stimulus becomes a conditioned stimulus and alone is sufficient to elicit the response. In Pavlov's experiment, he blew meat powder into the mouth of a dog, causing reflex salivation. The saliva was collected via a fistula in the cheek and the volume was measured. It was found that a standard quantity of meat powder would cause the secretion of a regular amount of saliva. Pavlov termed the meat powder the *unconditioned stimulus* (UCS) and the resultant salivation the *unconditioned response* (UCR). If a bell was rung immediately prior to the introduction of the meat powder, after several trials, the ringing of the bell alone would initiate salivation. Pavlov now termed the ringing of the bell the *conditioned stimulus* (CS) and the resultant salivation a *conditioned response* (CR). It was essential that the CS precede the UCS. If the stimuli were presented in the opposite order, conditioning did not occur.

Operant Conditioning

At the turn of the century, an American psychologist, Edward

Lee Thorndike, outlined the general principles of operant conditioning. Thorndike's "Law of Effect" stated that learning occurs if the response has some effect upon the environment. If the effect of the response is pleasant, then the behavior will be strengthened; whereas if the effect is unpleasant, then the behavior will be weakened. Thorndike initially worked with cats, chickens and dogs, which he placed in specially designed problem boxes and observed their escape reactions.

While still a graduate student at Harvard University, B.F. Skinner continued Thorndike's work and developed his well known "Skinner Box" for experimental behavioral studies in rats. The Skinner Box contained a lever, which, when pressed, caused a food pellet to drop into a feeding tray. The rat was starved for about 24 hours and then placed inside the box. Initially, the feeder was operated by the experimenter and the rat was allowed time to find the food pellets and eat them. Very soon, the rat became conditioned (via classical conditioning) to the sound of the feeder and would immediately run to the food tray. At this stage, a lever was connected to the feeder so that the rat had to operate the lever itself in order to receive its food reward. Characteristically, the rat would commence to explore the box and perhaps inadvertantly depress the lever, causing the feeder to deliver a food pellet. The rat would recognize the sound of the feeder and immediately run to the food tray to find its reward. After several trials, the rat became conditioned to regularly press the lever (operant behavior) for food reinforcement.

Classically conditioned respondent behaviors depend on an already existing reflex that is elicited by a preceding stimulus, whereas operant behaviors occur spontaneously as part of the animal's normal repertoire of behavior. Moreover, the frequency of a respondent behavior depends on the frequency of the eliciting stimulus, whereas the frequency of an operant behavior and negative reinforcement or punishment will suppress it. Although it is generally assumed that there are underlying differences between classical and operant conditioning, in practice these phenomena represent separate parts of the same stimulus-response paradigm and both concepts are equally important in training.

Some natural learning situations may be considered as a direct product of *classical* conditioning. In very young puppies, urination is normally evoked by the mother licking the anal and genital region. Without stimulation, urination is extremely difficult and the puppy's bladder will fill up. Later in life, urination may be elicited by other stimuli, such as the sensation of a full bladder or a full stomach. To some extent, the puppy learns to urinate voluntarily. As the pups grow older, a host of environmental stimuli may also begin to exert some controlling effect. Urination may be elicited by strange odors from other dogs and animals, as well as prominent visual landmarks, such as lampposts and fire hydrants. In other situations, the principles of *operant* conditioning appear to be important. A newborn puppy is rewarded by warmth and comfort for approaching its mother and it similarly receives an immediate food reward once it locates a teat. However, if the pup bites the teat too hard, the mother may respond with a cautionary growl or even a reprimanding nip.

Young dogs can be conditioned to urinate only at the time and in the place convenient to their masters. This Bulldog gets positive reinforcement from its owner when it urinates on newspaper during the early phase of housetraining.

Classical and operant conditioning techniques are equally important when employed during domestic training. The principles of operant conditioning are instrumental in regulating the frequency of any given behavior. Thus, if a dog receives food while begging at the table, it will increase the likelihood that it will beg at subsequent mealtimes. Similarly, if a barking dog is let inside, it will be more persistent with its vocal blackmail in the future. Alternatively, if the same dog worries the paper boy or mailman and is immediately clobbered with a copy of *The New York Times,* it will be less likely to exhibit such obnoxious behavior on similar occasions. The main function of classical conditioning is to form associations between a particular behavior and a relevant command. All dogs can sit, stay, lie down, and come, etc., of their own volition but in the process of training, these actions become associated with appropriate commands, so that the behavior of the dog may be predicted and controlled by the owner.

Generalization and Discrimination

When a dog has been conditioned to respond to one stimulus, initially it may generalize to other similar yet inappropriate stimuli, although in such instances, the response may not be as reliable or intense. For instance, a dog trained to bark at the door bell may occasionally bark when the phone rings. Gradually, the dog will learn to discriminate between stimuli, and responses which are not reinforced will be selectively extinguished whereas encouraged behaviors will be preserved.

The ability of a dog to make fine discriminations may help to explain some unusual behavior patterns. Consider for example a dog whose entire training program consists solely of one conscientious hour a week at a formal training club, and whose owners fail to comprehend his "Jeckyl and Hyde" nature. The dog is amazingly obedient while in the training ring, but as soon as the lesson is completed, the dog is out of the door chasing cats and children, and totally ignores or fails to respond to any command from the owner. The dog has simply learned that it must be obedient in a particular place at a particular time, when the professional trainer is present. For the rest of the week, the dog may, and often will, behave as it likes. It is advisable to train the dog at different times and in as many different situations as possible; in the house, in the garden, in other people's houses and on walks in the town and country, where there are a variety of distractions.

Some dogs may similarly discriminate between commands from different members of the family. The dog quickly learns that when mother says "no" it means "no," whereas three "no" commands from father may mean "maybe," "in a minute" or "do as you please."

Chaining of Stimuli

Pavlov demonstrated that via the process of classical conditioning, the sound of a bell would elicit salivation in a dog. Pavlov also noticed that after several trials, some dogs would commence salivating as soon as they entered the laboratory. In this sense, the previously neutral environment has become a conditioned stimulus. Examples of chaining of preceding stimuli are fairly common in the domestic environment. A dog will soon learn to come for its meal when called. However, within a very short time it may make the association between the sound of the can opener and the prospective meal. As time progresses, the dog may begin to respond to even earlier cues, such as the sound of the opening of the cupboard containing cans of dog food, the owner going into the kitchen and so on. Similarly, the chink of a choke collar and lead or the sight of the owner putting on hat and coat quickly become associated with the likelihood of an imminent walk.

In many respects, the dog has a better sense of time and place than his human companions. If a dog is regularly fed once a day at 6:30 p.m. when the owner arrives home from work, and is walked at 11:30 in the evening shortly before the owner retires, even without cues from the owner, the dog is aware of the time of day and may commence salivating before the meal is due and become restless prior to the walk. Often, it is these characteristic anticipatory behaviors that remind the owner that a pet dog requires food and exercise.

Secondary Reinforcement

In the same way that preceding stimuli may become linked together by association, reinforcers may become similarly associated. It is possible to train a dog with food rewards and painful punishments as *primary* reinforcers. However, it would be extremely inefficient and tiresome to either feed or physically punish the dog after each behavior. Instead, the use of *secondary* reinforcements substantially facilitates training, and makes the ordeal considerably easier for both parties. While petting the dog, or immediately prior to feeding, make the habit of saying "good dog," or other suitable terms of affection and approval. Very quickly the praise alone will serve as adequate positive reinforcement. Similarly, the words "no" or "bad dog" may be associated with punishment. It will only take occasional couplings of primary and secondary reinforcers to ensure the durability of the latter. Vocal approval or disapproval will be as effective as a food reward or physical punishment in controlling behavior. Thereafter, training sessions may proceed smoothly and efficiently without the need of dog biscuits or implements for torture.

138

Positive or Negative Reinforcement?

It is often asked which is more effective when training a dog, positive or negative reinforcement. The reason this question is so often clouded with heated controversy is that the two techniques have come to represent two very different schools of training: the *"natural method"* and the *"force method."* Also, both points of view have their own particular notion concerning what positive and negative reinforcement should represent. Negative reinforcement may vary between a fairly gentle reprimand, on one hand, to a very severe whipping on the other. Similarly, positive reinforcement may range from a terse vocalization of approval to three or four times the dog's weight in chocolate. An extreme exponent of the "force training method" might consider a reward to be the absence of punishment, whereas via the "natural method," negative reinforcement is often the absence of positive reinforcement. It would be naive to insist that either extreme is totally advantageous and a complementary combination of both techniques will presumably produce the best results. It is certainly easier, quicker and considerably more effective to train a dog via the "natural method," using only positive reinforcement. Nevertheless, in its lifetime, a dog will inevitably develop a variety of bad habits or undesirable traits, some of which are best prevented by immediate punishment.

The timing and severity of punishment largely determines its effect upon behavior. The effect is greatest immediately following the punishment, but in time the behavior often returns to its original level. This is the main disadvantage when using negative reinforcement for efficient behavior control. Punishment is useful for reducing the incidence of an undesirable trait, but in order to be continually effective the punishment must be continued periodically. If the dog is allowed to indulge in the bad habit, the reinforcing consequences of the behavior will override previous aversive conditioning. Occasionally, a dog may respond at an even higher level than before.

These principles have some important practical implications. It would be ridiculous to assume that short term correctional behavior modification by a professional trainer is going to permanently alleviate undesirable behavior traits. Punishment may temporarily decrease the behavior while the trainer is present, but unless the owner continues a similar training schedule in the home, the behavior stands a good chance of rapidly recovering. If ever the situation should arise where a professional trainer is necessary to correct bad habits, the owner should realize that this is not the fault of the dog. It isn't the fault of the trainers either, that such extreme methods are necessary; after all, they have a job to perform as quickly and efficiently as possible, since the owner would be certainly unwilling to pay larger sums of money for a longer lasting training program. The owner is entirely to blame for the unpleasant circumstance. Unfortunately, once this state of affairs has arisen, it is often a complete waste of time and money to take the dog to a specialized trainer. If the owner has been negligent in the original training program, it is unlikely that the necessary remedial treatment will be continued in the home. Despite an abrupt and temporary alleviation of symptoms, the behavior of the dog will rapidly deteriorate to the original level.

Schedules of Reinforcement

Reward. It is not necessary to reinforce every single occurrence of a behavior. In fact, continuous reinforcement schedules are relatively uncommon outside of structured experimentation within a laboratory setting. However, this should not be confused with consistency. An owner should always be consistent when giving commands, and insure that in every instance a particular command produces the appropriate response and that response only. The more common types of intermittent reinforcement schedules employed in training procedures are fixed and variable ratio schedules. In a fixed ratio schedule only one of a certain number of responses is rewarded, thus every third response might receive reinforcement. A variable-ratio schedule requires that the number of responses required for a single reinforcement varies from reinforcement to reinforcement in an irregular sequence. These reinforcement schedules may appear to be academic but differences between them have important practical implications. Under the influence of a variable-ratio schedule, the frequency of the operant behavior rapidly increases and then remains at a very high and nearly constant rate. Once the operant behavior has been acquired and maintained on this schedule, it is extremely resistant to extinction, compared with other schedules of reinforcement. In some ways this is extremely fortuitous for the trainer, who would find it difficult to adhere to a fixed schedule. This phenomenon is of importance during training procedures to facilitate the learning and retention of new behaviors. When using a food reward, it is best to commence training with a continuous reinforcement schedule until the dog has acquired the particular behavior. Then, gradually increase the number of responses that are necessary for a single reward. The conditioned behavior will be less easily forgotten and will be retained for a longer period of time, than if reinforced continuously. However, it also explains how easily superstitious behaviors may be acquired and why they are so difficult to extinguish.

To illustrate the difference between *fixed-* and *variable-* ratio schedule, consider both a vending machine, which delivers a packet of M&M's every fourth nickel, and a slot machine, which makes payments at random. The latter is considerably more fun and is much more likely to retain the attention of its user. Nonetheless, many vending machines, (for instance, the coffee machine on the third floor of the psychology building at Berkeley), appear to disperse potables according to a variable-ratio schedule. Perhaps this is the reason that it attracts such a large crowd of regulars.

Crime and Punishment. There are numerous forms of punishment; the majority involve the infliction of some kind of physical pain. One of the best is a quick hit with the hand accompanied by an expression of disapproval. It is advisable not to shout at the dog when scolding it, simply saying "no. . .bad dog" in a normal voice. This way, the dog will learn the words as secondary negative reinforcement, rather than relying on the tone of the trainer's voice. Briefly shaking the dog by the scruff of its neck is also very effective with the large breeds, perhaps because this is one of the ways that a bitch will reprimand her puppies. It is imperative that punishment is inflicted as soon as possible, and preferably at the very time that the dog is misbehaving. Methods of punishment such as electric goads, whips, brooms, rolled newspapers, dark closets and buckets of water are not readily available at a moment's notice, and consequently are largely a waste of time.

The temporal aspects of negative reinforcement cannot be over-emphasized. Even so, on many occasions, they are all too often abused. Perhaps one of the worst examples of inopportune timing of punishment is the instance of a dog that runs away from its owner when out for a walk in the park. The owner becomes exasperated from shouting for the dog and when the dog eventually returns, he is welcomed back with nothing but a barrage of insults and even a bit of aggravated NR (negative reinforcement). In such cases, the dog has not been reprimanded for running away but instead, it has been punished for returning to its owner! On many occasions, punishment is inflicted when it should not have been used at all. There is very little point in hitting a dog that has urinated or defecated on the carpet. This is simply punishing the dog for performing a necessary physiological function. Similarly, it is hardly fair to throw a bucket of cold water over a copulating canine couple. (Once they have locked it is too late anyway.)

Superstition

In the normal process of training, the changes in behavior are the result of deliberate manipulations. A dog is conditioned to salivate at the ringing of a bell, since it forms an association between the sound and the food reward. Similarly, a dog may form natural associations between occurrences that are dependent on each other. For instance, a dog quickly learns that the sound of a doorbell invariably heralds the arrival of visitors. Occasionally, however, associations may be formed by chance and the dog may be accidentally conditioned. If for example, the owner steps on the dog's tail in a hurried attempt to answer the doorbell, the dog may form an association between doorbell ringing and tail pain although the sequence of these two occurrences is contingent; the relationship was possible but improbable. Superstitious behaviors are true contingencies and develop from the chance reinforcement of behaviors. In this example, the unexpected negative reinforcement may be sufficient aversive conditioning to make the dog wary of the sound of the doorbell in the future. With domestic dogs, superstitious behaviors develop surprisingly frequently, and they are often quite difficult to extinguish, because they are the result of variable-ratio reinforcement schedule. Consider the over-loved pet that is given chocolate drops every few minutes. Each chocolate drop reinforces the preceding behavior. Thus, reinforc-

142

ed behaviors increase in frequency, and the prospect of their further reinforcement also increases.

Deconditioning

The ease with which a behavior may be deconditioned depends on how well it is established; that is, it depends on the frequency and magnitude of previous reinforcements and the type of reinforcement schedule. It is much more difficult to extinguish a habit that has been established by occasional or partial reinforcement, than one that has been maintained by continuous reinforcement.

There are several methods available to decondition particular behavior patterns should they be considered undesirable traits or habits:

a) removal of the eliciting stimulus
b) continuous presentation of stimulus without appropriate positive reinforcement
c) negative reinforcement
d) drug treatments

Some behaviors may be rapidly extinguished by simply removing the eliciting stimuli. Unfortunately, even after a long period of time, a single reintroduction of the offending stimulus often causes spontaneous recovery of the bad habit. For this reason this method is neither particularly effective nor advisable. For instance, should the dog have a penchant for biting postmen, the problem may be avoided by having the mail left outside the garden. However, should Western Union have to deliver a telegram, the delivery person will soon be thinking in terms of a lawsuit for damages. In such cases, the owner has decided to accept the bad habit and is trying to prevent it, or at least ignore it, rather than attempt to find the underlying cause and exercise a suitable cure. Very soon the various behavioral quirks and idiosyncracies of the dog begin to dictate the life of the owner. If the dog bites other dogs, they are kept away. If the dog suffers from car sickness, it is never taken in the car. If the dog dislikes people, the owner will live the life of a recluse. These are but a few examples.

In some households, it is impossible to utter such words as "walk" or "dinner" without the dog dissolving into an excited frenzy and insisting that it immediately be fed, or walked around the block. Some owners even resort to spelling out these words . . .

"Shall we take Rover for a w-a-l-k?" However, in no time at all, Rover will learn to spell. If the owner enjoys these antics, fair enough, but it would be much easier to say "walk, walk, walk, walk, walk" and then sit down and read the newspaper. After several repetitions of the stimulus without the appropriate reinforcement, Rover will soon learn to discriminate between the irrelevant "walk" and "Rover walk," which has the utmost pertinence to Rover. Another example would be the dog which superstitiously associates bells ringing with tail pain. If the bell is rung several times without being associated with pain, the superstition is soon extinguished as the dog learns that the bell ring is an irrelevant stimulus.

Dogs that are gun-shy or afraid of thunder and lightning may be similarly cured. When the puppy is quietly playing in the sitting room, put Tchaikovsky's *1812 Overture* on the stereo at low volume. Once the pup is accustomed to the music, activate an occasional flash bulb in a corner of the room. If the puppy seems unperturbed, gradually turn up the volume and occasionally direct a flash at the puppy. If the pup appears apprehensive, decrease the volume until it is comfortable at that level and give the puppy plenty of attention while increasing the volume further. This should serve to acclimate the pup to loud bursts of noise which may occur in the future.

If the dog has acquired bad habits that are particularly offensive to the owner, necessitating rapid deconditioning, negative reinforcement may be the only solution. In such instances, the timing of the punishment is the most important consideration. If the dog has stolen a chop from the table, there is no point in administering punishment afterwards, since it is unlikely that the dog will make a retrospective association between the crime and punishment. The dog must be punished *in the act,* or better still, reprimanded when it is *about* to misbehave. In the normal course of events, this is exceedingly difficult, and in all practicality improbable if not impossible. To facilitate the deconditioning procedure, it is ad-

Opposite: The Afghan Hound, a breed dating back to antiquity, has been trained through the ages to "work" in the capacity of a coursing hound. Today, such coursing trials are gaining in popularity.

visable to structure a tempting situation which will increase the likelihood that the dog will misbehave, so that reprimand and/or punishment may be administered at the correct time. In the above example of the "supper thief," set up a delicious smorgasbord on the table and then sit down in a comfortable chair and reprimand the dog each time it shows any intention of stealing a quick lick of a roast. It is important that the food on the table is large enough so that it can not be swallowed in one gulp, or else quick action on behalf of the dog will reinforce the opportunist foraging behavior. Oxtails are ideal, especially if the meaty end is temptingly dangled over the edge of the table. Even if the dog does get hold of the bone, it may be pulled from its grasp before he gets the reinforcing bite of meat. If the trainer is afraid of being bitten in this exercise, tie a piece of string to the end of the bone. Once this stage has been achieved and the dog will not attempt to touch the food while the owner is in the room, tie the small end to the table leg and fix a bell on the string. Leave the end of the bone protruding over the table edge and retire to the newspaper and a comfortable chair in the adjoining room. At the sound of the bell, say "no, bad dog" and rush into the kitchen. The problem is solved. And from now on, do not leave unattended food within reach of the dog!

Similar tempting structured situations may be designed to cope with any problem. An additional and surprisingly helpful therapy is to recommence standard training sessions with simple commands like "sit," "lie down" and "come here," etc. It is difficult to say why this is so effective. Perhaps it helps the dog to attend to the owner, and as such, be more responsive to his wishes, or perhaps it merely relieves some of the monotony of everyday domestic life.

In extremely acute or severe cases that are particularly resistant to deconditioning, sometimes drug therapies have proved to be efficacious. These treatments usually involve heavy tranquilization or even prolonged anesthesia. However, their effectiveness is limited without an accompanying sensible retraining program, and as much as possible, the owner should try to counter a behavioral problem with a behavioral treatment.

Prevention is better than cure
From the outset, it should be realized that there is no domestic

dog that is untrainable. On the other hand, there are numerous owners who find it impossible to train their pets. There are certainly a great deal of individual and breed differences in temperament, but despite these genetical predispositions and early behavioral traits, the training schedule employed by the owner will have an overriding influence on shaping the resultant behavior of the dog. The subsequent emergence of various behavioral quirks and annoying canine habits are almost entirely the fault of the owner, and they are not an expression of some congenital idiosyncrasy of the dog. What should be a relatively simple training program is all too often muddied by lack of forethought by the owner. Not only does the owner fail to recognize maladaptive traits while they are developing, but quite often they are unintentionally encouraged.

Many people will accept a puppy into the home without a thought of the responsibilities or practicalities that are involved. They are often surprised when their cute little puppy gets bigger and starts to eat twenty dollars worth of food a month, and the occasional turgid veterinary bill invariably comes as a dire shock. Feeding and caring for the dog's physical health should be part and parcel with the enjoyment of having a canine companion. One should consider whether there is sufficient space to keep the dog, adequate time to look after it properly and whether there are sufficient funds to meet unexpected medical bills, as well as routine husbandry costs. Another important consideration is a wise choice of breed to suit the home and budget, in addition to personal preferences. It is best to reflect on these factors before acquiring a dog, rather than having a retrospective enquiry as to why intentions were valid but the dog was unsuitable.

It is a good idea to imagine the puppy as a full grown dog and treat it accordingly from the beginning. Would one want an eighty pound Malamute lounging in the best armchair? Or is the dog's principal vocation to be an excavator of pansies or an ingestor of furniture? If urine stains in the garden or chewed parking tickets and tax returns are the normally accepted way of life, then that's fine, but if this sort of behavior is unwanted from an adult dog, the puppy should *never* be allowed to do it. Although it is very tempting to afford a lovable puppy greater license for misbehavior, and to consistently make exceptions because "it's so cute," it must be

147

remembered that these bad habits are much easier to prevent during puppyhood than they are to cure at a later date. It is up to the owner to decide the dog's prospective position in the household and to start the puppy off accordingly. Is it going to be outdoors all the time, inside all of the time, or inside some of the time but upstairs none of the time? There is no need whatsoever to physically punish the puppy but one must be very firm concerning those behaviors that are condoned and those that are forbidden.

It may be extremely amusing to have a fluffy puppy bundling up the stairs and jumping on the bed, but this is not quite so humorous when the puppy has grown into a 120 pound St. Bernard. If this is to be allowed at any time, then it should be allowed all the time. If the adult dog is not going to be allowed upstairs, then do not allow the puppy upstairs. The variable-reinforcing schedule of giving the puppy an overdose of attention sometimes, but chasing it down the stairs at other times when it is inconvenient for the puppy to come into the bedroom, will often cause problems should the owner decide to decondition the dog and train it not to come upstairs. (Moreover, when it is inconvenient for the puppy to come into the bedroom, it is often inconvenient to chase it downstairs. The best solution is not to allow the puppy upstairs in the first place).

A similar example is the puppy that is constantly worrying people at the dinner table. If feeding at the table is to be condoned at all, the puppy should be fed once and only once. To try to ignore the pup's attentions in an attempt to impress dinner guests, only to become softhearted after half an hour of paws and whines and eventually slip the puppy a quick potato, will only reinforce an intensely annoying behavior, which will be extremely resistant to extinction later on. Again, the easiest and simplest solution would be to never allow the dog in the dining room at meal times from puppyhood onwards. Be consistent.

It is inconvenient for the owner, and certainly unfair to the dog, if the latter is not trained. Owners, hopefully, convey instructions to their dog, but the dog fails to understand simply because it has not been *trained* to understand. Often the owner will get frustrated and annoyed, and the dog will be punished and confused. A dog cannot be expected to comprehend complex and heuristic commands, nor should the owner suffer the misapprehension that they can miraculously establish a magical empathic understanding with the dog. (Even so, most dogs certainly try their best to glean much information from the owner's tone of voice and mannerisms as well as from other more subtle and inadvertent cues, whereas human skill in this respect is somewhat inferior). The best way to communicate with the dog is via very simple and distinct commands that can be taught in a very short time by elementary training techniques.

The most important principles in training are forethought, consistency, simplicity and patience. Bearing these in mind, the entire process will be easier for both the owner and the dog.

TRAINING SESSIONS

It is not a good approach to wait until the dog is fully grown and then expect to do wonders with an hourly training session each

If you want your adult dog to be as well-mannered as this Afghan Hound appears to be, begin training early on, with short but frequent exercise periods.

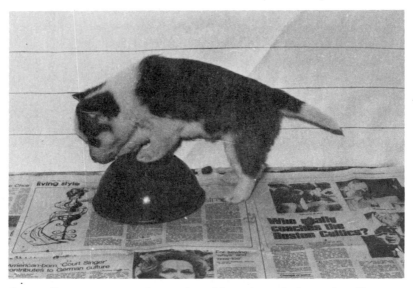

Soon after your puppy has eaten, his enlarged stomach will exert pressure on his bladder and colon and he will have to relieve himself.

week. Training should begin as early as possible, as soon as the puppy comes into the home. Of course, very little can be expected from a puppy that is only six or seven weeks old, but even at this early age, it is possible to start housetraining and to familiarize the pup with acceptable and non-acceptable behaviors by encouraging the former and discouraging the latter.

The formal training sessions should be short but frequent. If they are too long, both the puppy's attention and the owner's patience deteriorate and the situation becomes worse than hopeless. At the start, just five minutes before each meal is sufficient. Usually at this time, the puppy's attention is directed wholly towards the owner. If not, the dog is not hungry, and training will be facilitated if the pup is not fed for a couple of hours. As the dog grows older, it is advisable to vary the time and place of training sessions. One of the main difficulties in training is commanding the puppy's attention. Normally a dog is tuned to the social signs and signals of other dogs and not to human beings. Many of these principles have been outlined in the chapter on socialization whereby the dog optimally becomes adequately socialized toward both dogs and humans and will soon learn to look toward its owner for food and affection, (both of which may be used as useful bribes when training).

Another consideration is a suitable method of communication by which the dog may understand, or at least be aware of the trainer's commands and wishes. A dog would normally rely on olfactory information, vocalizations and visual cues. However, it would be inconvenient, although not impossible, to attempt to duplicate the relevant canine sounds and body postures, or for example to instruct the dog to be seated using a variety of odors and ear positions. Instead, it is more practical to teach the dog to attend to human vocal commands. It is irrelevant to the dog which particular commands are used. There is very little difference whether the dog is trained to stand to the command "sit" or *vice versa*. It is largely for the owner's convenience that the commands are meaningful. However, it is extremely important that the commands are distinct, not ambiguous, and easily discriminable. There is little point in mumbling commands, such as "now please sit down and please your owner, there's a good doggie," and expect the dog to respond; it will have great difficulty in discriminating the relevant words. Instead, the command should be "Rover sit." Both the dog's name and a clear and firm training voice are advantageous in attracting the dog's attention. There is no need to shout; the dog can hear quite well.

HOUSEBREAKING

A young puppy will reflexively urinate and defecate in response to the mother licking the anus and genital areas, and the bitch will generally consume both urine and feces. As soon as the puppy is a few weeks old, it achieves some degree of voluntary control over its elimination functions and if at all possible it will avoid soiling its own bed. The pup will want to relieve itself about half a dozen times a day and given the opportunity, it would much prefer to do this out of doors, so that it has the chance to investigate the various odors left by itself and other neighborhood dogs. These natural tendencies make house training a fairly simple process, although some owners still hold the view that they have been responsible for a major accomplishment.

During the initial stages of housebreaking, it is advisable to confine the puppy to a single room, preferably one with a nonporous, easy-to-wipe floor. A convenient puppy box may be made from a large open-topped cardboard box that may be obtained from an appliance store. Cover the floor of the box with newspaper and in one corner place a smaller box that is just small enough for the puppy to curl up inside. At nighttime, leave the puppy in the box and first thing in the morning take the puppy outside so that it may urinate. The next step is to give the puppy the first meal of the day. The grossly enlarged stomach will exert pressure on the bladder and colon and the puppy will soon be in need for relief. This is an ideal time to play with the pup for a short while, always keeping an eye open for the slightest indication of imminent elimination, so that the pup may be quickly taken outside. The puppy very quickly learns the house rules, and will wander toward the door when it is in need.

An alternative method is to cover the entire floor with newspaper. As soon as the puppy becomes accustomed to using the paper regularly, the area of the floor covered by the paper may be gradually reduced until it is the size of a single sheet, preferably located near the door. At this stage, the paper may be put outside with just a corner showing under the door. The puppy will attempt to use this small piece and will characteristically paw and whine at the door, which is a convenient signal that it is time for "walkies." For the first few visits outside, the procedure may be facilitated by taking a sheet of paper to put down on the grass as an added stimulus. Each day, halve the size of the paper until to all intents of purpose, it disappears.

COMMANDS

From the outset, a puppy should understand three things: its name, "good dog" and "no. . .bad dog." Its name should be used as a prefix to all commands, first to attract the puppy's attention and second so that it may easily recognize and discriminate those commands intended for the dog. Otherwise, what is the purpose of giving a dog a name? In addition, as soon as the puppy comes into the home, the owner should attempt to regulate behavior with "good dog" and "bad dog." When feeding or petting the dog, "Rover, good dog," and when interrupting a behavior that is not allowed, "Rover, no . . . bad dog." Very simple; which is the easiest way the puppy will learn to understand your meaning.

The degree to which a dog should be trained will vary from dog to dog, depending upon its particular station in life. The purpose of training is to facilitate the dog's adaption to the home environment, in such a manner that owner and dog may entertain a mutually enjoyable relationship. However, commands such as "sit" and "come here" are absolutely essential and should be taught to every domestic dog, whereas it is only necessary for the dog to learn to respond to "lie down," "stand," "heel" and "stay," if it is frequently walked without a leash. An untrained dog is a menace if allowed on public property. For this reason, each command will be discussed separately. Should the training

From the outset, it is essential that a puppy should learn to understand three things: its name, "good dog" and "no, bad dog."

A dish of milk provides a chance for some harmless play for these Afghan Hound puppies. But think about training them before they grow into adults.

schedule become an enjoyment rather than a chore, the owner may wish to embark upon a more sophisticated program. Suitable recreational or "luxury" commands will only be discussed briefly.

"Come Here"

Many owners have great difficulty in getting their dogs to come when called. Surprisingly, this is one of the easiest commands to teach. There are three basic approaches: the feeding method, the armchair method and the picnic method. *The secret is to begin early.* First, make a point of heralding each and every meal with the cry 'Rover, come here." Miraculously, Rover will soon come running. Once this response is well established, change to a comfortable armchair in the living room sometime before the puppy's supper. Once in a while, call the puppy and occasionally reward it with a small amount of affection, or a small dog biscuit. That is all it takes. The pup will soon realize that an obedient visit to the owner promotes adequate compensation. The next step is to take the puppy along on a family picnic to a strange area, preferably to a field or park where there is little likelihood of being disturbed. As the puppy explores the surroundings, it will frequently return

154

to the owner for reassurance before embarking on a slightly more adventurous exploration. The trick is to wait until the puppy is just about to return from an exciting foray into the unknown, and only then give the command to come. The puppy will eagerly return. When this response is well established, train the pup to sit by the owner's left side before giving suitable reinforcement. During the initial stages, only call the puppy if there is a likelihood that it will obey. If it is otherwise occupied, do not bother. Try not to run after the pup, this will be too much like an enjoyable game.

"Sit"

A puppy may be trained to sit in a very short time, especially if it is rewarded for sitting of its own volition. The technique is to design a situation in which one knows that the dog is going to sit down, so that it may be commanded to do so beforehand and rewarded immediately afterward. It is easiest to hold the first few lessons on a corner table, which prevents the dog from running away, and saves the backbreaking problem of bending down to puppy level. It is easier to do all training with a hungry puppy using individual pellets of the dog's standard dry dog food as a reward. Hold the pellet just above the puppy's nose and slowly move it backwards. The dog will shuffle back into the corner and then raise its head and sit down in order to take the food reward. Command the puppy to "sit" just before it begins to go down. Do not let the dog snatch the food; hold it firmly in the fingers and only let it go when the dog is prepared to take the pellet gently. Repeat this about ten times a day and in about three or four days, when the puppy begins to respond regularly, perform the exercise on the floor and only reward every second or third response. Command the dog to sit in a variety of situations; it is a good idea to always make the dog sit while its food is being prepared, and to remain seated in front of the food bowl for a short while.

"Lie Down"

Command the puppy to sit on the table and, as before, present a food pellet, but this time hold it just under the puppy's nose. Slowly move the pellet downward so that it comes to lie just below and a little in front of the table top. At the same time, give the command "lie down" and the puppy will lie down to take the pellet. After ten or so trials, repeat the procedure on the floor us-

ing an intermittant reinforcement schedule by selecting only the best responses for reward.

"Stand"

To train the puppy to stand is also a relatively easy procedure. When it is sitting or lying down, hold the food reward a little in front and above the puppy's head and say "stand" when it begins to get up. When lying down the puppy will sometimes go into the sitting position but as it leans forward to take the food, the hindquarters will lift off the table.

"Heel"

Hold a food pellet in the left hand and walk at a fairly rapid pace and a hungry puppy will follow with its head level with the trainer's left hand side. Stop occasionally and command the dog to sit and donate a food pellet toward only the better responses. The entire sequence of behavior is being rewarded and soon the dog will walk to heel and automatically sit when the trainer stops. From the start, it is better to train the puppy to "come" and to "heel" without using a leash and only with positive reinforcement. Otherwise, a dog soon learns to discriminate between situations in which it must obey because it is wearing a lead, and alternative situations when it does not have a lead and consequently will be less likely to obey.

"Stay"

Once the dog is sitting, instruct it to lie down and then walk backwards a few yards repeating the command "stay." After a short pause, return to the dog and reward it in the lying position. Alternatively call the dog to "come" and give a food pellet when it arrives. If the dog decides to follow the owner or otherwise disobey, walk toward it and repeat the procedure. Punishment is not necessary. Gradually it is possible to retreat greater distances and to leave the dog for longer periods. Then try to walk out of the room and repeat the command "stay" until out of sight and then immediately return and reward the dog. At first, keep the intervals very short. It is worth taking the time and trouble to design a few

Opposite: To teach the "stay" command, once your dog is sitting, take a few steps backwards and repeat the command. After a pause, return to the dog and reward it with a food pellet and words of encouragement.

tempting situations to test the dog's obedience. For example, make the dog lie down and stay in a corner of the living room, place a large oxtail a couple of feet in front of its nose and retreat to a comfortable distance but keep a good eye open. If the dog attempts to move even an inch, repeat the command. It is important that the dog learns to remain in the spot designated. It is a good idea to teach the dog to stay in both the lying down and the sitting positions. Most obedience trials require the dog to lie down but this is not such a good policy on the pavement outside a bank or supermarket, where people are apt to trip over dozing dogs.

"Don't Touch"

This is a very useful command. Put a large oxtail in front of the dog and command it not to touch. If it shows any movement toward the bone, repeat the command or even slap the ground beside the bone with a rolled newspaper. If in the early stages of training the dog manages to grab the bone, it is imperative that it be expropriated immediately. This is why it is important to use a large oxtail. A small scrap of meat or cheese would disappear from view before the wag of a tail and then it would be too late for punishment. If the dog is allowed to get away with it just once, the entire cause is jeopardized.

This is an extremely useful command for the dog to understand and even easier for the dog to learn. Life can be much easier if the dog has been instructed not to touch human food, knitting, games of chess, cats, babies and old ladies, etc.

"Be Quiet"

To make this job easier, do not get in the habit of actively encouraging the dog to bark, unless upon command. Never feed a dog or let it come inside to stop it barking. Otherwise, it is being rewarded for making a noise. When the dog is happily barking away, give the command "be quiet." If it obeys, demonstrate your approval a short while later. Sometimes ordering the dog to "lie down" and then "be quiet" has a better effect. It is more difficult for the dog to bark when lying down. If it barks again, approach quickly and repeat the command in an utterly convincing and somewhat annoyed tone, while looking straight into the dog's eyes. If it barks again, try not to laugh, but instead shout the command once more and tap the dog on the nose and perhaps give it a

Never let a dog come inside the house to stop his barking. Otherwise, he will be rewarded for making a noise.

quick shake by the scruff of the neck. Never let the dog have the last say. Even reprimand the pianissimo bark which inevitably occurs about ten minutes later. If the dog is outdoors and does not respond to the command, rush outside screaming "be quiet" and throw a rolled newspaper, or anything handy that might accentuate the trainer's mock rage. This has to be convincing, since the dog must not find the procedure enjoyable. Then return indoors and repeat the charade if the dog should bark again. Once the dog is beginning to get the idea, place the emphasis on the command rather than the tone or emotion.

In many households, one of the functions of the dog's bark is to herald the arrival of expected and unexpected visitors and this sort of behavior needs to be encouraged. After a couple of barks have signalled some corporeal presence, first indicate approval: "good dog," etc., and afterwards signal the dog to lie down and cease barking.

There should be no excuse for having a domestic dog debarked. This is a costly surgical remedy for a simple behavioral problem. It is about as absurd as cutting the legs off a dog that runs away. If a dog has to be debarked, it is really an admission of the owner's incompetence. If the barking is consistently annoying the neighbors and the owner is incompetent and can neither train the dog nor convince the neighbors to move, then debarking may be considered as an alternative to having the dog euthanized. The operation is quite humane, but in the majority of cases, it should simply be unnecessary. The dog still enjoys going through the actions of barking and there is no evidence to suggest that the lack of noise production has any deleterious effects on the dog. The dog will happily continue to bark with fewer decibels; however, it is pitiful to watch.

"Bark" or "Speak"

Once it is possible to successfully command the dog to stop barking, it is safe to train the dog to bark on command. To elicit a bark, take the dog to a strange place; for instance, shut it in an empty garage, and give the command to bark. When the owner is out of sight, the dog is likely to bark immediately. Return with lots of affection and perhaps a food reward. After a few repetitions, the dog will soon learn this very easy and enjoyable exercise, after which the command to bark may be given each time the doorbell rings or whenever somebody opens the garden gate. After a few barks, instruct the trained guard dog to be quiet. A barking dog is an excellent deterrent against burglars. To prevent the possibility of an intruder poisoning the dog with baited meat, it is possible to train a guard dog to only accept food in certain situations: from its owner, from its feeding bowl and only after a specific signal, such as "Rover, eat." With the help of a few friends masquerading as would-be intruders, it is easy to train the dog to bark if offered food under any other circumstances.

Many people, especially those that live alone, keep a dog for protection and often consider having it professionally trained for attack purposes. In the first instance it is better for the owner to do the training personally, but once a dog has been trained to attack on command, then it should *always* be under the supervision of the trainer-owner. With the exception of specialized police dogs and military dogs, this is usually impractical. It is a far safer idea to train the dog to bark or growl upon command. Whether the particular command to growl happens to be "speak," "defend," "attack," "kill," "destroy" or "mutilate" will have little relevance to the dog, but it will unquestionably provide a meaningful deterrent for a potential mugger or rapist. If the command is constantly repeated in an agitated tone, the dog will usually build itself up into an excited frenzy. For the unfortunate attacker, the prospect of anything but a rapid retreat will seem forbidding to say the least.
160

Two faces of an Alaskan Malamute. Despite the wolf-like features, the Malamute is no more closely related to the wolf than other domestic breeds, such as the Poodle and Chihuahua.

"Fetch"

Teaching a dog to retrieve is fun for the owner as well as the dog. A well trained dog can become quite adept at retrieving golfballs, or even be a useful asset as a twelfth man in a game of cricket. At the same time, the dog will be enjoying well needed exercise.

When the dog is playing with its ball, wait until it has picked it up in its mouth and then offer a food pellet and catch the ball as the dog's mouth opens. Then roll the ball away from the dog and repeat the procedure. After a few successful trials, instead of approaching the dog, let the dog bring the ball before it is given its reward. In a very short time, the dog will be eagerly waiting for the ball to be thrown again.

Once the dog has mastered the art of retrieving it can be used to teach the dog a large vocabulary and discriminate between objects. This has unlimited practical applications ... "fetch paper," "fetch slippers,' "fetch pipe," "fetch grandpa," etc.

Other Signs and Signals

When the dog is thoroughly accustomed to the relevant verbal commands, it may be trained to obey silent dog whistles or hand signals. If nothing else, this is a lot of fun for the owner and never fails to impress onlookers. The whistle or hand signal should be given immediately prior to the verbal command and the dog rewarded for the correct response. After only a few pairings of the stimuli, whistles or hand signals alone will suffice.

The silent dog whistle should be calibrated to a known frequency so that it may be replaced if lost. Whistles of differing frequencies may be used to command different dogs. The specific signals are for the owner's choosing but suitable examples are shown below. The signals that involve the animal remaining at a distance all commence with a short blast of the whistle and the signal "come here" is the only one that starts with a long blast. Suitable hand signals are also described.

Command	Whistle	Hand Signals
Sit	two short blasts (..)	one arm raised
Lie Down	one short and one long (.-)	motion down with one arm
Stay (Wait)	one short and two long (.--)	two arms raised
Stand Up	two short and one long (..-)	motion up with one arm
Come Here	Three long (---)	beckon with one arm
Heel	etc.	clicking fingers

7. Origins of the Dog

CLASSIFICATION OF CANIDAE

Our best friend, the domestic dog, is a carnivorous mammal. Today there are seven families of modern land carnivores: bears, dogs, raccoons, weasels, civets, hyenas and cats. Counting pandas as a separate family, there would of course be eight.

Dogs are mainly carnivorous and live in most parts of the world. They have four toes and are digitigrade (i.e. walk on small pads under their toes). As such, they are well adapted for swift running on open plains and usually run down their prey after an enduring chase, finally seizing it with their long jaws. In fact, African wild dogs can maintain speeds of about thirty miles an hour for a distance of up to three miles, after which they usually give up the hunt if the quarry has not yet been caught.

Bears are five-toed and plantigrade; that is, they walk on the soles of their feet. They are generally omnivorous, feeding on berries, nuts, tubers, insects, and, to a lesser extent, on flesh. Usually, they live in forests or in rough mountainous country. Like bears, raccoons are omnivorous forest dwellers, and are mainly arboreal, living in trees. They have five toes and are semi-plantigrade. With the exception of one Asiatic genus, they are all New World animals.

Weasels are also five-toed semi-plantigrade animals and they have extremely flexible bodies. They are usually forest dwellers, more strictly carnivorous than dogs and they have specialized shortened jaws for seizing and holding their prey. Civets are similar in adaption but within the family there is considerably more diversity of specialization. They are natives of the Orient and Africa and are unknown in the New World. Hyenas are four-toed, digitigrade, and have massive jaws. They are inclined to feed on carrion and sick animals. Members of the cat family are carnivorous in diet, hunt primarily by stealth and ambush their prey

Above: A male dog normally performs a thorough investigation before urinating. However, urine marking is not the sole prerogative of male dogs. Opposite, above: Many females may also spend considerable time investigating the surroundings before directing their urine towards specific visual and olfactory stimuli. Opposite, below: Adult male dogs do not always employ the full leg elevation posture. When urinating in the open they may lift their legs to a varying degree.

165

with a sudden burst of speed. They seize the prey with sharp, retractile claws and hold on with their jaws, instead of snapping and slashing as dogs would. They have four toes on the hind feet and five on the fore feet. They are nearly as cosmopolitan as members of the dog family but as yet have not reached Australia.

Domestic dogs along with their wild counterparts wolves, coyotes, jackals, foxes and the so-called wild dogs of South America, all belong to the genus *Canis* of the dog family *Canidae*. There are four other genera in this family each having a single species. The classification of Canidae has been based on the number of digits on fore and hind legs and on the number of molar teeth. Foxes have sometimes been included in a separate genus *(Vulpes)* largely because their foot pads are hairier and the tail is longer and bushier. There are also differences in behavior, but nonetheless, the Arctic fox is very similar to some species of wolf, and for the purpose of this chapter, the Mivart classification is adhered to, and foxes are included as members of the genus *Canis*.

EVOLUTION OF CANIDAE

From the fossil record, it appears that modern carnivores have evolved from small insectivorous animals. In the evolution of *Canidae* in particular, the transition from the original forest dwelling ancestors has been characterized by an adaption for swift long distance running, for hunting down prey, along with changes in dentition necessary for seizing and eating the victim.

The earliest mammals appeared as much as 150 million years ago in the Mesozoic era, at a time when giant prehistoric reptiles were abundant. The reptilian dominance lasted for over one hundred million years and ended fairly abruptly some sixty million years ago, leaving primitive mammals to fill the ecological vacuum. At that time, mammals were small brained, largely insectivorous and were probably egg-layers, much like present day monotremes (duck-billed platypus, echidna, etc.). They were covered with hair, presumably developed from reptilian scales and could maintain their body temperature to some degree, although most likely they still hibernated in the cold winter months. Ancestral carnivores (*Creodonta*) appeared at the end of the Cretaceous period and from these the first of the *Miacidae* evolved in the earliest Tertiary formations.

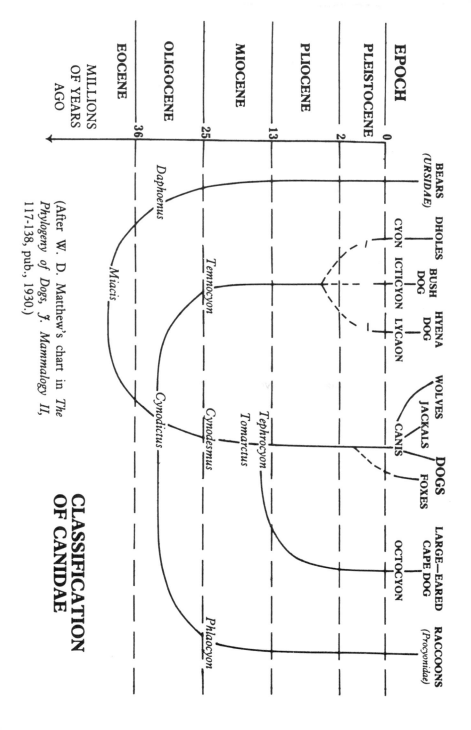

CLASSIFICATION
OF CANIDAE

(After W. D. Matthew's chart in *The Phylogeny of Dogs*, *J. Mammalogy* II, 117-138, pub., 1930.)

EPOCH	MILLIONS OF YEARS AGO
PLEISTOCENE	0
PLIOCENE	2
MIOCENE	13
OLIGOCENE	25
EOCENE	36

BEARS (*URSIDAE*)

DHOLES — CYON

BUSH DOG — ICTICYON

HYENA DOG — LYCAON

Daphoenus

Temnocyon

Miacis

Cynodictis

Cynodesmus

Tephrocyon
Tomarctus

WOLVES
JACKALS — CANIS
DOGS
FOXES

LARGE—EARED CAPE DOG — OCTOCYON

Phlaocyon

RACCOONS (*Procyonidae*)

1

2

(1) Newborn pups will snuggle close to the bitch in an effort to keep warm. (2) The bitch will lick the pup's ano-genital area in order to stimulate elimination. (3) After consuming a meal, a litter of Husky pups commence suckling for dessert. (4) The bitch tears at the umbilical cord of a newborn pup.

3

4

It is thought that there was only one genus of *Miacidae* in the Paleocene and this was presumed to be the time when the specialized carnassial, or flesh-eating teeth first evolved. In the Eocene, there were certainly numerous species of *Miacidae*, all with characteristically differentiated carnassials and molars, which had been partly converted into crushing teeth. *Miacis* was the typical genus and most authorities assume that it provided the ancestry of present day dogs, bears and racoons. It was a small civet-like carnivorous mammal with short legs and a long body. The limbs, feet, and skeleton closely resembled those of present day arboreal carnivores. In the Oligocene, two important genera had evolved from *Miacis*. Their bodies were still sleek and long and had a closer resemblance to modern weasels and civets than dogs. They were five-toed and had partially retractile claws, which were ideal for their partly arboreal forest existence. The larger of these, *Daphoenus* was about the size of a coyote and rather fox-like in proportions with a long heavy tail. In the early Miocene *Daphoenus* resembled a bear-dog, much like the present day wolverine; it later became very large in size and evolved into the bears in the late Pleocene. The smaller *Cynodictus* is thought to be the ancestor of the dog family and its teeth resembled those of modern canids.

In the Miocene *Cynodictus* gave rise to three important genera: *Phlaocyon*, which is thought to be the ancestor of the racoon family; *Temnocyon*, which is represented today by the hunting dogs of Africa and India and perhaps the bush dog of South America; and *Cynodesmus*, from which wolves, coyotes, jackals and foxes have evolved. In the transition from *Cynodesmus* to *Tomarctus* in the late Miocene, the legs and feet became longer and the thumb and big toe were lost. The inner digit became vestigial on the hind foot and considerably reduced in size on the fore foot. With the lengthening of the limbs and the pronounced digitigrade method of locomotion, the canid ancestors became better adapted for running at high speeds. The tail became smaller in size and the body proportions came to resemble those of modern wolves and foxes. In fact, it has been suggested that foxes can be traced back to small slender-jawed canids of the Upper Miocene, hardly distinguishable from *Tomarctus*, which is generally regarded as the common ancestor of the wolf and coyote.

As land-living carnivores began to prey on larger animals, pairs of carnassial teeth evolved. They are self sharpening and act like shearing blades for cutting tendons and stripping flesh from bones. Carnassial teeth are most prominent in dogs, cats and hyenas as well as in some of the weasels and civets. In the dog family they comprise the fourth premolars in the upper jaw and the first molars in the lower jaw. In addition, the canine teeth have become enlarged and pointed. Fossils of wolves, coyotes, jackals and foxes may be found in the Pleistocene that are essentially similar to their present-day descendants. In the Old World, coyotes were replaced by jackals, especially in Oriental and African regions.

ORIGIN OF THE DOG

The question of the origin of the domestic dog has remained a much-debated and intriguing problem for many years. Charles Darwin addressed himself to this dilemma in 1897 in his book *The Variation of Plants and Animals under Domestication*. At that time, these were two main points of conjecture. First, it was debated whether the dog was domesticated at several times in a variety of places throughout the globe, or whether it was domesticated only once and thereafter spread all over the world. It was suggested that the dog was initially domesticated in Central Europe and the Middle East and subsequently spread in a northeasterly direction through Eurasia to the Americas and also southward to Africa and Australia. Second, it was considered whether the varieties of domestic dog were descended from a single wild species or several. Some held the view that the dogs' single ancestor was a wolf or jackal or even some unknown extinct species. Despite these suggestions, the favorite tenet at the time was that domestic dogs had a multiple ancestry consisting of species both extinct and extant. The concept was originally put forward by Pallas in 1780 and its main support was the amazing anatomical variation between the breeds. However, Darwin later pointed out that this could easily be accounted for by the effects of selective breeding, as may be seen by the great differences between races of domestic animals which certainly descended from a single ancestral form.

Isidore Geoffrey Saint-Hilaire (1860), perhaps the first true ethologist, considered that there was no constant difference be-

171

Above: The Australian Terrier is thought to have descended from a cross between Yorkshire and Dandie Dinmont Terriers.

Opposite: The German Shepherd Dog was originally used as a dual purpose animal. In addition to its function as a sheepherder, the breed also proved to be an effective watch dog.

Thousands of years ago the wild ancestors of our modern day domestic dog began their association with humans, when they scavenged about human cave dwellings for food. This modern-day Beagle, peering out from its own seeming "cave dwelling," probably bears little resemblance to its wild ancestors.

tween the structure and habits of jackals and some of the smaller races of dogs. He also thought that some breeds of dogs had originated from wolves. The idea of a jackal ancestry was strongly disputed by Cuvier, head of the *Academie des Sciences* of Paris in 1810, who objected that "The jackal would not have been domesticated on account of its offensive smell." However, the degree of odor varies greatly among the different varieties of jackal, and anyway, it does not seem likely that olfactory esthetics would have been the primary consideration of humans in 8000 B.C.

Nonetheless, Darwin was much in favor of the multiple ancestral theory, and suggested that domestic dogs were descended from: at least two species of wolf, (the Northern and the Prairie wolf (coyote), and maybe other European, Indian and North African varieties); several races or species of jackal; one or two species of South American canines and perhaps even one or more extinct species. He also mentioned the possibility that as domestic dogs were introduced they might have crossed with already existing aboriginal *Canidae* in the country. Darwin covered most options but was careful to add:

We shall probably never be able to ascertain their (domestic dogs) origin with certainty. Paleontology does not throw much light on the question, owing, on the one hand, to the close similarity of the skulls of extinct as well as living wolves and jackals, and owing, on the other hand, to the great dissimilarity of the skulls of the several breeds of domestic dogs.

Darwin further added that perhaps the only solution would be to let the various pedigree breeds of dog become feral and interbreed at random. Under such conditions, the inbred characteristics would disappear and the dogs would revert to their ancestral form (a phenomenon known as *atavism*).

Darwin was certainly quite correct in at least one assumption: that the true ancestry of the domestic dog would most probably remain a mystery. Even today, it is about as clear as the paternity of some neighborhood mongrels. However, this uncertainty has in no way stemmed the introduction of a vast number of favorite theories on the subject.

Up until the 1930s it was generally considered that dogs originated from species of jackals that had been crossed with other wild *Canidae* both living and extinct. This view was later promoted by Konrad Lorenz in his popular book *Man Meets Dog* (1954), in which it was suggested that the golden jackal was the first dog to be domesticated by man. An important reason for implicating the jackal or even the coyote was their smaller size. However, one of the main effects of domestication has been the selective breeding for smaller forms and there has been a gradual diminution in size from the wild type. Lorenz was well aware of other possibilities and added that:

> . . . we do not know for certain that it was exclusively the golden jackal (*C.aureus*) that attached itself to man in the way described. It is indeed very probable that in different parts of the earth, various larger and wolf-like species of jackal became domesticated and later interbred . . .

Later in the book, Lorenz acknowledges the dual origins of dogs from both wolves and jackals but still maintains the impression that the jackal ancestry is more important. Soon the controversy developed into the "wolf/jackal" debate, although in the light of

Above: The Alaskan Malamute, once a hardy worker for the Mahlemuit Indians, has adapted to a more easy-going lifestyle in our modern civilization.

Opposite: A St. Bernard dam and her young pup.

recent behavioral evidence, Lorenz withdrew his suggestion of jackal ancestry in favor of the now generally accepted notion that the dog was domesticated principally from one or more species of wolf. Nevertheless, it is impossible to say for certain that jackals, coyotes and other wild *Canidae* played no part, especially since it is known that the jackal still breeds freely with pariah, shenzi and dingo-like dogs, in much the same way that some northern breeds, such as Huskies and Malamutes may be backcrossed with wolves.

The dentition, skull formation and other anatomical characteristics of the domestic dog closely resemble those of the wolf. Likewise, the behavioral patterns and various other phenomena such as the duration of pregnancy, the blind period of the young, the moulting phenomenon and the order of appearance of the milk teeth are identical in both wolf and dog. This raises the possibility that the various races of the domestic dog descended from a single wild species, the Northern Timber wolf. It has even been suggested that because of their close similarity, the domestic dog may be considered to be a form of wolf and not a separate species.

Since the time of Darwin, the most comprehensive and realistic approach to the question of the ancestry of the domestic dog is that offered by Richard and Alice Fiennes in their delightful book *The Natural History of Dogs* (1968). They said that:

> ... the anatomy of the skull emphasises the essential oneness of wolves, coyotes, jackals and wild and domestic dogs. It supports the view that the more primitive dogs, such as the dingo, huskies, basenjis, and pariahs are very closely related to wild canid ancestors and indeed cannot in any scientific sense be separated from them. It also supports the supposition that jackals are merely wolves, which have taken to a different way of life and have thus come to develop qualities suited to it within the original genetical constitution.

The book traces the origins and dispersal of the different breeds of dog from ancient and classical times. The Fiennes suggest that the domestic dog has not been derived from a single stock but instead, the parent stock, which is undoubtedly wolf, may also have been crossed with the jackal or other wild *Canidae*. Despite these complications, the authors proposed that domestic dogs may be

178

classified into four main groups, each of which they feel indicates a separate wolf ancestry:

1. *The Northern Group* derived mainly from the Northern wolf (*C. lupus*) including Huskies, Malamutes, Samoyeds, Chow Chows, Collies, German Shepherds, Corgies, and terriers.
2. *The Mastiff Group* derived from mountain wolves such as the Tibetan wolf (*C. lupus chanco* or *laniger*), including Great Dane, St. Bernard, Mastiff, Newfoundland and the true hounds and gun dogs.
3. *The Greyhound Group* derived from a more cursorial wolf ancestor related to the pale-footed Asian wolf (*C. lupus pallipes*) or perhaps the smaller desert wolf of Arabia (*C. lupus arabs*), including Wolfhounds, Borzois, Salukis, Afghan Hounds, Greyhounds and Whippets.
4. *The Dingo Group* derived from the pale-footed Asian wolf (*C. lupus pallipes*) and including Basenjis and Rhodesian Ridgebacks.

The Northern Group

This group contains the sledge dogs: Huskies, Malamutes and Samoyeds, sheepdogs such as the German Shepherd and Collie and hunting Spitz dogs such as the Elkhound. In addition, perhaps the large terrier group should also be included. It is generally accepted that the large grey Northern wolf (*C. lupus*) or its American counterpart, the timber wolf, was the main ancestor of the northern breeds of dogs. However, some breeds may have been affected by crossing with jackals or even domesticated dingo types which migrated northward. Sled dogs from the far north such as Huskies and Malamutes are probably closest to their wolf ancestors. The Malamute is thought to have originated in Alaska some 3000 years ago from the working dog of the Mahlemuit Indians. It is said that Eskimos will tether their Husky bitches while they are in heat, so that they may be backcrossed with wolves in order to keep the breed tough and hardy. The curly tails, characteristic of Elkhounds, Samoyeds and even perhaps Malamutes have been derived from crossbreeding with dingo-pariah type dogs of the Finno-Ugrian peoples, who were thought to have migrated northward into Finland from the Volga region of

The modern day English Setters were bred by Edward Laverack and during the nineteenth century were originally known as Laverack Setters.

The Weimaraner was thought to have been descended from the Bloodhound. At the end of the eighteenth century they were bred at the Weimar Court and were originally used for hunting big game.

Certain breeds have long been identified with royalty, such as the Pekingese with Oriental monarchs. Cardigan Welsh Corgies have long been favorites of Queen Elizabeth II of Great Britain. Here, one is seen in a royal family portrait, circa 1959. Photo by Sport and General Press Agency, London.

Russia. A smaller variety of the Spitz-Elkhound group may have given rise to the Welsh Pembroke Corgi, which was brought to Pembrokeshire by Flemish weavers in the early 1100's and used as a cattle dog. (Cardigan Corgies have a more disputed ancestry and are thought to be derived from Dachshund stock which was probably brought to Wales by the Celts in the 12th century B.C.)

Other northern breeds have developed outstanding abilities as sheepdogs and shepherd dogs. The purpose of a sheepdog is to round up selected sheep for penning, whereas this is a secondary function of shepherd dogs, whose main purpose was to protect the flock from wild animals and robbers. The Collie is certainly the most skilled dog for working sheep but in the more northern European countries where wolf attacks were not uncommon, the German Shepherd (Alsatian) was much preferred. (In England following World War I, the *Deutsche Schäferhund* [German Shepherd Dog] was renamed the Alsatian wolf dog, inferring that it had originated in the province of Alsace rather than in Germany proper.) Skills that the German Shepherd lacked in working sheep were easily compensated by its superior fighting ability that better enabled it to defend the flock.

The origin of the large terrier group is rather obscure but in all probability they were derived from Spitz dogs such as the Elkhound. The terriers, as their name implies (*terre*, in French, means ground) were used to follow foxes and badgers to their below-ground quarters and flush them out. As such they were small, compact and highly courageous. Some breeds were also used for hunting small vermin such as rats or mice.

The Chihuahuas are also included in the northern group. They were most probably descended from the Techichi, a heavily boned long haired dog kept by the Toltec Indians in the ninth century. After the Aztecs conquered the Toltecs in the 16th century, they adopted the dog and crossed it with a hairless variety.

The Mastiff Group

Characteristically, the mastiff breeds have fairly short muzzles with a pronounced stop between the nose and forehead. They also have long soft coats and floppy ears, which probably evolved as a protection against the cold. All the breeds in this group originated

183

Above: The Boxer originated in Germany. It was bred from Mastiffs used as cattle dogs and watch dogs, which were thought to have been crossed with a strain of English Bulldog.

Opposite: The Dalmatian and Dachshund, two breeds with widely different backgrounds, share a harmonious existence in the same home. The Dalmatian's precise origins, while somewhat unclear and subject to different interpretations, point to a past history as a coach dog. The Dachshund was bred for hunting badgers.

185

from the great mountain chain that stretches westward across Europe from the Pyrennes in the Iberian peninsula to the Himalayas and the mountains of Tibet. They are descended from the woolly coated mountain wolves such as the Tibetan wolf (*C. lupus chanco* or *laniger*). It seems likely, however, that part ancestry of some breeds may lie with the Asian wolf of Northern India, and there may be evidence of some Spitz or pariah blood.

Primarily, the mastiffs were used as shepherd dogs and were presumably descended from the huge Molossian and Hyrcanian hounds that were used to guard the flocks of the Molossi and Hyrcanian tribes of Greece and the southern shores of the Caspian. Mastiffs were also used by the Assyrians as war dogs and these no doubt gave rise to the great Newfoundland, Pyrenean, St. Bernard, Great Dane and mastiff breeds of today. All the mastiff type dogs have acute powers of smell and this group is the origin of the true hounds and modern day gun dogs.

The mastiff was brought to Britain by Phoenician traders in the 6th century B.C. The breed was well established by the time the Romans invaded in 55 B.C. and was used to fight the invaders. Later they were used to fight in Roman amphitheaters. The most famous strain was bred at Lyme Hall in Cheshire and represents a pure line since the 15th century. There are many anecdotes concerning the Lyme mastiffs. When Sir Peers Lee was wounded on the battlefield at Agincourt, his body was supposedly guarded by a mastiff which had followed him to the war.

The St. Bernard was originally bred by the monks of the Hospice St. Bernard, which is situated in the Alps, above the St. Bernard Pass. The dogs were used to locate people lost in the snow.

Despite its name, the Great Dane (Grand Danois) almost certainly originated in Germany and was formerly known as the German boar hound (*Deutsche Dogge* or *Ulmer Dogge,* after the town of Ulm in Würrtemberg). It is a fast-moving, lively dog due to its part Greyhound ancestry. It was either bred from crossing Mastiffs with Greyhounds or Bloodhounds with Irish Wolfhounds. Nevertheless, the Great Dane retains its fine sense of smell and does not normally hunt by sight.

The Bloodhound of today is probably the closest relation to the ancient Molossian and Hyrcanian mastiffs. They were descended

186

It is almost certain that the Great Dane originated in Germany, where it was known as the German Boar Hound. True to their Greyhound ancestry, Great Danes of today, such as this Harlequin (white with black patches) are fast-moving and lively.

Above: A field-trained spaniel enjoys the spoils of a hunting excursion. As the name suggests, the spaniel type originated in Spain.

Opposite: The Black and Tan Coonhound is well known for its ability to tree racoons.

from the hounds of St. Hubert that were indigenous to the Middle East. They were introduced into France in the sixth century and were taken to England in the tenth century. Their name is popularly thought to be derived from their ability to follow a trail of human blood and in the days of yore, they were frequently used to track down runaway slaves and convicts. Bloodhounds gave rise to other breeds of hounds, all of which use their sense of smell while hunting: Foxhounds, Beagles and Harriers (for hunting hares), Otterhounds, Basset Hounds (*bas*, in French, means low) and Dachshunds (badger hounds).

The gun dogs have probably been bred from spaniels (*Spanielle*, from Spain). It is likely that the larger breeds of spaniel were descended from smaller varieties of Pyrenean mountain dogs, whereas other spaniels may have come from primitive forms of pointers.

Poodles are thought to have been derived from the same ancestors as water spaniels. Originally, Poodles were used for retrieving game from water. The Poodle's coat contains lanolin, which helps make it water resistant (the coat of the Newfoundland is similarly oily). The characteristic grooming of the Poodle was meant to add buoyancy to the front of the dog, yet leave the rear legs free so that they could work better in the water.

The Greyhound Group

There is some controversy concerning the origin of the name Greyhound. It may have been derived from Greekhound (*Graiushound*), or alternatively from gazehound, because the dogs hunted primarily by sight, or perhaps because they were used to hunt down gazelle. It is thought that the greyhound type dogs originated from some more cursorial ancestral variety of the pale-footed Asian wolf. All members of this group are characteristically long-legged with a sleek body and long, pointed noses. They are extremely fast and normally run down prey primarily by sight, rather than tracking the scent. The Greyhound group largely originated in the Middle East during times when much of this area was fertile and harbored an abundance of wild game. It seems likely that in these open lands a more cursorial variety of the pale-footed Asian wolf might have developed, which later became extinct as the fertile hunting grounds turned to desert as recently as 7000 years ago.

190

If in fact, this wolf-like ancestor did exist, then its domesticated form is preserved today in the form of the Saluki, probably one of the oldest pedigree breeds of dog. The name Saluki is thought to be derived from the Arabic word "slughi," which means respected or venerated dog. This is most probably a reflection on its impeccable pedigree, comparable to that of the pure bred Arabian horses. Another possibility is that the derivation comes from the Greek Seleucid empire, which flourished in the Middle East some 2000 years ago. The Saluki was the hunting dog of the Arabs and was trained to run down, catch and detain the prey until the master arrived and killed it in the fashion prescribed by that particular religious faith. Afghan Hounds were found farther north in the mountainous lands of Afghanistan. Their much longer coats protected them from the colder environment.

Borzois, or Russian Wolfhounds, were used in pairs for hunting wolves in Imperial Russia. They were bred by crossing the Tartar Greyhound with Russian Laikas, which were used for boar hunting and looked very much like Samoyeds. Irish Wolfhounds and Scottish Deerhounds were probably descended from a common stock of Celtic war dogs, which were introduced into Great Britain over 2000 years ago.

When Lord Orford founded the Greyhound Coursing Club in 1776, he strengthened the breed by crossing it with the Bulldog. The English Greyhound was used for coursing a variety of wild game. However, nowadays, only the hare is used.

More recently, Greyhound racing has become increasingly popular. For each race, six dogs are simultaneously released from their traps, to chase an electric hare around the track.

The Dingo Group

Dingoes are wild dogs thought to be derived from the pale-footed Asian wolf, and apart from size there are very few differences between dingoes and wolves. Although there is the possibility that the dingo may have been aboriginally introduced to Australia by man, the similarity between the dingo and extinct forms of dog suggest that this introduction must have been ancient. Here, of course, there is the possibility that a domestic variety of dog may have reverted to the wild state and subsequently underwent re-domestication. The term "dingo" is really Australian, but the dingo group represents the semi-wild dogs that are

The Alaskan Malamute is a very old breed which had its origins as a working dog of the Mahlemuit Indians.

scavengers from human settlements. In Africa, they are known as shenzi dogs and in India and the Middle East as pariahs (which supposedly ate the body of Jezebel, the Biblical figure who was the evil wife of Ahab, the King of Israel).

When the Europeans settled in South Africa, they crossed their domestic breeds with shenzi or kaffir dogs and new breeds such as the Rhodesian Ridgeback were evolved. The Basenji, which very much resembles a dog of ancient Egypt, was re-discovered in Sudan and Zaire.

The advent of sheep farming in Australia led to a drastic reduction in the number of dingoes, which nowadays are only to be found in central Australia around aboriginal settlements, or in Queensland. A domesticated form, the Queensland heeler is used for rounding up cattle.

Behavioral and Morphological Plasticity

In St. Georges Mivart's *Monograph of the Canidae* (1890), he classifies the wolf, coyote, jackal, fox and domestic dog within a single genus, *Canis*. Although all members may have their own particular characteristics, there are no distinguishable anatomical features that would justify their separation into different genera, and the different groups would appear to gradually merge into each other. There is anatomical evidence to suggest that the northern wolf shades indistinguishably with the Tibetan wolf, the Tibetan wolf merges with the pale-footed Asian wolf and this in turn with the desert Mesopotamian wolf. Moreover, there is little difference in size or any other obvious features between some of the larger jackals *(C. aureus)* and the Mesopotamian and other smaller breeds of wolf. These wolves and jackals may interbreed and produce fertile offspring. This trend may extend to other groups. The coyote is often termed a Prairie wolf and similarly smaller species of jackal are identical to types of foxes.

It is known that domestic dogs will interbreed with wolves, coyotes, jackals and foxes and produce fertile offspring, whereas the disparity in size between some breeds of dog makes it impossible for them to mate. Similarly, there is more variation between the skeleton of a Chihuahua and a St. Bernard than between any wild type of *Canidae*. Despite this, few attempts have been made to separate domestic breeds into different species. Recognition of the extreme variations between the domestic breeds facilitates the understanding of why wolves, coyotes, jackals and foxes all belong to the same genus. Fiennes and Fiennes have emphasized the fact that there are no basic physical or behavioral differences between the different types of Canids:

> . . . the various attributes seen in the various groups of *Canidae* are therefore part of a single genetical spectrum, of which one part is emphasized in one group, another part in another group; it can only be supposed that wolf-like animals could be bred in time from foxes and fox-like animals from wolves.

Thus, wolves, coyotes, jackals, foxes and domestic dogs are all part of the same genetical theme and share the potential for common canid behavior patterns. The range of behavior that is expressed by any particular group is determined in part by the type

A dog's range of behavior will be determined in part by the type of habitat in which it dwells. An environment that does not offer much in the way of companionship—human or otherwise—will cause a dog to become withdrawn, and not properly socialized.

of habitat colonized. Certain genetical traits may be suppressed, but are not eliminated, and emphasis may be given to other aspects of constitution and behavior which are best suited to the life style demanded by that particular habitat.

Canids have the behavioral flexibility to rapidly adapt their way of life to meet changes within the environment, without making any significant changes to their genetical contitution. Normally, wolves hunt their prey in packs, whereas jackals are scavengers and live on carrion, although they will also eat young birds, eggs, mice and insects, etc. However, should the conditions of available food supply change, jackals may revert to hunting in packs, whereas wolves will eat snails, slugs, other invertebrates and even vegetation and fruit, despite their obviously carnivorous dentition. The common fox in Britain fed mainly on the ready supply of rabbits until the outbreak of myxamatosis decimated the population, whereupon the fox changed its diet to include invertebrates, roots, carrion and even the occasional spoils from a raid on a poultry farm. Arctic foxes and timber wolves will eat fish. Animals which are dependent on a single type of food or habitat become more restricted. *Canidae*, on the other hand, have a cosmopolitan distribution, enjoying extremes of climate and a changeable variety of food sources.

Even among wolves, there is considerable individual variation of both physical and behavioral features. Fiennes and Fiennes have pointed out considerable differences between two skulls of northern wolves. One skull very much resembled the skull of a German Shepherd-Collie type of dog with an elongated muzzle, whereas the other tended towards the mastiff type, with a broad thick skull and a pronounced stop. The same variations seen within the species are also apparent even within a single litter, in which puppies are of many different sizes, colors and temperaments. It is this individual variation which has formed a basis of hierarchical structure and division of labor within the wolf pack and was one of the first stepping stones for canine domestication in various parts of the globe.

Patch   Dart   Gyp   Scamp

Tanya   Ken   Rio   Ollie

Sooner   Sacha   Tasha   Selene & Friend

Toa-Bie   Poosey & Dinky   Jezebel   Ivan

Bentley   Bundle   Dopey   Muffin

Many breeds of domestic dog are represented here in a number of poses and settings. All are animals that the author has owned or known over the years.

8. Domestication Of The Dog

When the intellectual gulf began to widen, in the author's fancy, the man stood on one side and the rest of the animals on the other. The man looked upward at the sky, and all the other animals walked off, each about his own business. "All, did I say? All but one! The little dog sat on the very edge of the widening gulf, ears cocked, tail moving, and watching the man. Then he rose to his feet, trembling. "I want to go to him," he whined, and crouched as if to leap.

The pig grunted and went on rooting in the ground; the sheep nibbled a tussock of grass; the cow chewed her cud in calm indifference. It was none of their business whether he went or stayed.

"Don't try *that* jump," said the friendly horse; "you can't possibly make it; I couldn't do that myself."

"Oh, let him try it," sneered the cat; "he'll break his silly neck and serve him right."

But the dog heard none of them; his eyes were on the man, and he danced on the edge of the gulf and yelped. And the man heard him and looked across and saw what he wished to do.

"Come!" shouted the man.

"I'm coming," yelped the dog.

And then he gathered himself and leaped. But the gulf was very wide—almost too wide for a little dog. Only his brave forepaws struck the farther edge of the chasm, and there he hung without a whimper, looking straight into the eyes of the man. And then there came to the man a strange feeling that he had never had before, and he smiled, stooped and lifted the dog firmly and placed him by his side, where he has been ever since. And this was the very beginning of the movement which, ages later, led to the foundation of the first humane society. And the dog went frantic with joy and gratitude, pledged his loyalty to the man, and he has never broken his pledge.

E.H. Baynes, *National Geographic,* March 1919

The domestication of animals by man is thought to have occurred in late Paleolithic or early Mesolithic times. It is generally assumed that the dog was the first animal to be domesticated and the earliest date cited is 18,000 B.C., but there is little evidence to substantiate this claim and perhaps *circum* 8000 B.C. would seem to be a more realistic estimate. An alternative view has been offered by a Swiss paleontologist, Professor Roth, who has suggested that the first animal to be at least semi-domesticated was a giant sloth, *Grypotherium domesticum.* There is even less evidence to support this. Nevertheless, in the National History Museum in London, there is a fossilized skeleton of an extinct giant sloth, which was found behind a wall in the back of a South Patagonian cave. At the end of the last century, there were occasional expeditions to South America in an optimistic attempt to locate living specimens.

Along with the dog, reindeer, sheep and goats were also domesticated early in Mesolithic times. The development of agriculture marked the advent of the Neolithic revolution, which encouraged the development of new relationships with other wild species. It is probable that herds of wild bovines and other herbivores might have regarded the fields cultivated by humans as ideal grazing, and these crop robbers, cattle, pigs and yak were soon to be domesticated primarily for meat and skin. Additional animals, domesticated for other reasons, primarily for transport and labor, were the elephant, ass and onager. Some animals were domesticated by secondary nomads in regions where agriculture was no longer profitable due largely to deterioration of the soil.

Nomads required a means of transport and in various regions the horse and camel filled these roles. As agricultural settlements became more developed, it became necessary to effect means to destroy pests and vermin. The cat, ferret and mongoose are the most prominent examples of animals that were domesticated for this purpose. Since that time a whole variety of other animals have been domesticated: the llama (American Indian), rabbit (Medieval Europe), hyena and gazelle (Egypt), various birds (chicken, turkey, goose, duck, etc.), silk moth, honey bee, fish and numerous pets. Recently, research has begun on the possibility of game farming in Africa. The idea is to keep various species of wild game, such as the eland, elephant and water buffalo, in a semi-domesticated state and cull bachelor males and suitable youngsters. Compared with domestic cattle, game species are not so susceptible to enzootic diseases of the tropics.

Reasons for Domestication

Various hypotheses have been put forward to explain the original purpose behind domestication. Among these is the theory of religious origin, whereby token animals were kept for ceremonial or religious purposes and gradually became tame, as they were bred in captivity. In many ancient civilizations, dogs assumed a religious or mystical significance. In ancient Eygpt, the Greyhound and Mastiff type dogs were highly venerated and some were considered sacred. The brightest star in the heavens was the dog star, Sirius, which is located in the constellation *Canis major,* and was considered to be a god and protector. The first appearance of Sirius above the horizon regularly heralded the annual overflowing of the Nile. The prosperity of Lower Egypt was dependent upon the irrigated fertile area around the Nile and soon Sirius symbolized friendly watchfulness and dependability. In ancient Egyptian religion, Anubis, regarded as a deity, played a significant role in the ceremonial funeral rites as the jackal-headed god of tombs and embalming. At a later date an entire city, Cynopolis (the city of the dog) was constructed in honor of Anubis.

In many cultures, the dog was regarded as the guardian of the home and generally acquired a spiritual and mystical significance. As long ago as 6000 B.C. dogs were reportedly buried with their

The Pekingese is a breed that dates back to antiquity and has been traced to the Chinese Tang Dynasty. This is a painting of "Lootie," one of the Pekingese that was brought back to England and presented to Queen Victoria, following the looting of the Peking Summer Palace in 1861.

masters in Eygptian tombs in order to ward off evil spirits. According to Herodotus, if a household dog died in ancient Egypt, the family members would shave their hair as an expression of grief.

From Egypt, dog worshipping spread to many other countries. In Greek mythology, Hades, the abode of the dead, was guarded by the three-headed giant Mastiff-like dog, Cerberus. The Romans also made sacrifices to Anubis and Procyon, the lesser dog star in the constellation *Canis minor,* which appeared before the dog star Sirius. (In Greek, pro means before, and kyon means dog). Many dogs were bred exclusively in monasteries and temples in Tibet and China. The Pekingese has an extremely long pedigree which extends back to the Chinese Tang Dynasty, and it is probably related to the Tibetan terrier, Shih Tzu and Lhasa Apso. It used to be known by a variety of names, "Lion dog," "Sun dog" (because of its golden color) and "Sleeve dog," because it was often carried around in the owners' voluminous sleeves. Later, it was named the Pekingese, after the Chinese city of Peking. The lion was supposedly tamed by the holiness of Buddha and the "Lion dog" was presumably bred because they were smaller and more manageable than real lions. (This is similar to the way that domestic cats found their way into Egyptian religion—because larger wild cats were too dangerous). Chinese Emperors were invariably surrounded by a host of these sacred dogs as an honor to the Lord Buddha. It was the custom for commoners to be put to death if caught in possession of one of the royal Pekingese. However, following the looting of the Imperial Palace, five Pekingese were taken to England as breeding stock in 1860.

In other cultures, the various canine deities assumed a more dubious reputation. In Celtic myth, Cernunnos was represented as a cross between a wolf and a stag. In Scandinavian mythology, Fenriswolf was a very nasty evil wolf and Garm was an enormous dog. Fenriswolf was descended from the giant Ymir, the spirit of evil. Three brothers, Odin, Vile and Ve, representing Spirit, Will and Holiness, killed Ymir and all the other giants drowned in his blood with the exception of Bergelmir, who escaped to father numerous children. Among these was Loki, who in turn fathered three terrible offspring, the Fenriswolf, the Midgard serpent and Hel, the goddess of death, who in conjunction with Garm were continually at war with Thor and the good gods. Odin was killed by the Fenriswolf, who in turn was avenged by Odin's son Vidor, who tore the wolf apart with the help of magical footwear.

In many cultures, wolves became totem animals of worship. In many ways totemism helps to explain the numerous werewolf legends. A werewolf is a person who has the ability to turn himself into a wolf. This supernatural or magical transformation is known as "lycanthropy." There was an outbreak of werewolves in medieval Europe, particularly in France, where they were known as *loups-garous*. The phenomenon has been connected with religious wolf cults, voodoo and insanity. (Virgil, the Roman poet, attributed lycanthropy to the effects of drug taking). According to Arcadian legend, the first man who inhabited that region,

Pelasgus, had a son called Lycaon, who sacrificed a human baby in honor of Zeus and was immediately transformed into a wolf. Since that time, a man has always changed into a wolf, following a sacrifice to Zeus. If the wolf does not consume human flesh, it changes back into a man after nine years, whereas if it has indulged in a bit of human, it then remains a wolf forever.

The presence of the dog in many religious and mystical ceremonies was certainly one of the main factors contributing to the initiation of the unique relationship between dogs and humans. With the inhabitation of permanent settlements, dogs entered into even closer relationships. They were allowed inside the dwellings as guard dogs and to control rats, mice and other vermin and, subsequently, they were accepted as pets. According to mythology, in 850 B.C. Odysseus, disguised as a beggar, returned to his house in Ithaca after ten years of wanderings after the Trojan war. His wife, Penelope, and sons Emmus and Telemachus failed to recognize him, but his faithful dog Argus knew its master immediately. If nothing else, this story tells us that at the time of Homer, dogs were kept as pets in the household.

There are a whole host of anecdotes concerning the faithfulness and fidelity of "man's best friend," the dog. One such legend concerns an Irish setter named Gelert, which was given to Llewellyn the Great, the King of Wales, in 1205 by King John of England. One day when Llewellyn was returning home from hunting after Gelert had deserted him in the field, he encountered the dog, covered in blood, coming from the gates of the castle. Llewellyn went to his son's room and saw that the bed was overturned and the bed linen stained with blood. He called for his son but there was no reply. The king assumed that Gelert has killed the boy and in a rage, Llewellyn plunged his sword into Gelert's heart. A further search revealed the child asleep behind the overturned bed next to the body of a large wolf that Gelert had killed. Llewellyn was filled with grief, and subsequently built a chapel in memory of Gelert and erected a tombstone over the dog's grave. Both of these may be seen today in the Welsh village of *Beth Gelert* (the grave of Gelert).

Another well-known story involves a Skye Terrier known as Greyfriar's Bobby, who was always seen around Edinburgh in the company of his master, Auld Jock. Following Jock's death and burial in the local graveyard, the dog slept on his master's grave for the remainder of his days. When Bobby died, a statue was erected in the center of town, commemorating his unfailing loyalty.

Many authorities have favored the impression that the tendency for women and children to keep pets was an incentive for initial domestication. The scavenging habits of wild *Canidae* inevitably brought them into contact with humans, and occasionally pups may have been adopted. In fact, folk stories of several African tribes have explained the domestication of the dog exactly in this way. Darwin has described several primitive peoples from all parts of the world, who still tame and rear wild animals, which would seem to support this idea. Moreover, there are still tribes in Southeast Asia and tropical America whose women nurse pups and piglets as well as their kids (both caprine and human).

Another suggestion is that domestication occurred primarily for economic reasons, since animals represented a ready supply of meat and skins. However, this is unlikely, since Mesolithic man would probably have found it far easier to hunt and trap for supplies when required, rather than having the burden of feeding and caring for captive animals. Instead, humans were most likely unaware of the implications of the gradual establishment of a loose social bond between animals and themselves. It seems that domestication occurred by accident, and it was not until much later that human realized the economic importance of domestic animals. In fact, considering the remarkable capacity that dogs have for associating with humans, it has even been suggested that rather than humans domesticating dogs, the converse may have been true, that our faithful friend actually domesticated us. From the dog's point of view, this may not be quite as silly as it sounds.

Considering the vast number of species in the world, it seems surprising that only a few have been domesticated. The choice of species was probably left to circumstance, and it has been only recently that specific animals have been intentionally domesticated for a particular purpose. Nevertheless, there are certain factors that have obviously increased the likelihood that a species would become a suitable candidate for domestication. The prime consideration is purely a utilitarian one and depends on whether the domestication of the animal would be in any way beneficial to the human society and the second factor is the ease with which the animal may be domesticated. For instance, it is favorable that the animal adapts well to a wide range of dietary and environmental conditions. Of course, an essential and obvious criterion influencing the suitability of a species for domestication is that they will breed well in captivity and are preferably promiscuous.

When breeding foxes for fur it is the accepted practice to only leave a male and female together for a couple of hours at the most, otherwise the dog fox may establish a permanent pair bond with his vixen and refuse to mate with other females.

It was previously thought that a social way of life with an hierarchical group structure was the essential criterion that determined the choice of species. However, the domestic cat proves to be an exception to this rule, since it was almost certainly descended from a distinctly solitary Egyptian species, *Felis ocreata*. It is certain that sociability is beneficial but it is not the only determinant. Darwin (1875) postulated that dogs receive humans as the leader of the herd or family and more recently Lorenz has fancifully extended his view when he talks about two origins of fidelity in his delightful book *Man meets Dog*:

> The dependence of a dog on his master has two quite distinct origins; it is largely due to a lifelong maintenance of those ties which bind the young wild dog to its mother, but which in the domestic dog remains part of a lifelong preservation of youthful character. The other root of fidelity arises from pack loyalty which binds the wild dog to the pack leader or respectively from the affection which the individual members of the pack feel for each other.

Domestication has not been restricted to humans and their animal subordinates. In his book *A History of Domestic Animals*, (1963), Frederick Zeuner has stated: "Man has applied the same practice to members of his own species, though in this case it is usually called slavery, unless a more euphemistic word is used." Also, humans are not the only species to practice domestication. In the animal kingdom, there are a variety of examples of symbiotic relationships between two species. True symbiosis is rare, when two species permanently live together in perfect harmony and both partners derive equal benefits from the relationship.

A loyal sentry: A statue of Greyfriar's Bobby in Edinburgh.

Usually it is an unequal relationship and one species subjugates the other. Scavenging may be an example of a true symbiotic relationship; one species receives food and the other benefits from the removal of waste products and food debris. According to Zeuner, an original mutually-advantageous overlap of the social media of two species is the first requisite for domestication. The guest/host relationship may remain in a voluntary and harmonious equilibrium, or in some cases, as if a bit of a good thing is not enough, one species may exploit the other. If the guest exploits the host, the relationship becomes parasitic, whereas, if the host exploits the guest, the relationship may develop in the direction of domestication or slavery. There are many instances of both types of relationship in the animal world. Two species of North American ant live in nests that are occasionally intertwined. The smaller ant (*Leptothorax emersoni*) may enter the galleries of the larger one (*Myrnica canadensis*) but not *vice versa*. The *Myrnica* are not hostile to their smaller neighbors, but instead seem to regard them with tolerant indifference. The *Leptothorax* are social parasites; they lick the *Myrnica* and beg food and are rewarded with regurgitated drops of food juice. Another ant, (*Polyergus rufescens*) keeps slaves. The species will raid the nests of *Formica fusca* and kill any resisting workers and capture the young. The *Polyergus* return to their nest and hand over the *Formica* pupae to resident *Formica* slaves, who bring them up as "faithful servants of the colony." *Polyergus* have become dependent on the slaves to such an extent that all domestic duties in the colony, even nest building, are conducted solely by the slaves, while *Polyergus* restricts its activities to making the occasional raid.

Stages of Domestication

Zeuner has described several phases in the process of domestication:

1. Overlap in the social media.
2. Breeding in captivity (sexual isolation).
3. Selective breeding for particular traits.
4. Extermination of wild ancestors.

Originally, there was an overlap in the social environment and loose contacts were established between animals and humans. Wolves would scavenge around human settlements (one authority has suggested that they were attracted by a plentiful supply of human feces). Occasionally, humans would frighten wolves away from a fresh kill, and at a later stage smaller and younger individuals were captured and the puppies grew up in captivity and interbred in sexual isolation from the wild type. The process of domestication was well underway before humans realized the economic potential of the domestic stock and began to consciously breed for specific beneficial traits. Once domestic breeds had become standardized, they were so different from the wild ancestral species that interbreeding with wild *canidae* was highly undesirable, since it would dilute the domestic characteristics that had been laboriously selected. For this reason, (and others), the wild ancestors were gradually exterminated. In this respect, it seems somewhat ironic that domestic breeds, such as the Irish Wolfhound and Borzoi (Russian Wolfhound) were used for this purpose. However, it is interesting to note that in Australia, the wild dingoes are in danger from extinction primarily because they are interbreeding with the domestic breeds.

The domestic dog has been used and bred for a wide variety of functions. The hunting exploits of humans were aided by the superior senses and abilities of dogs to track down and kill prey. Their natural herding propensity was employed in hunting as dogs were used to drive herds of animals over cliffs or towards men with spears and bows. Even today, some African tribes use dogs to drive wild boar into nets whereupon they are killed with spears. Dogs were also employed for herding reindeer, caribou and sheep, with the additional function of guarding the flocks from wild animals and robbers. In the north, dogs were used for draught purposes for pulling sledges. In various parts of the world, dogs have been killed for food and their skin used as clothing.

As the forests and wolves had been systematically destroyed progressively northward, dogs were not required for controlling wild animals. Similarly, with improvements in agriculture, most of the land was under cultivation. Instead, the sporting element of hunting assumed popularity, at least for those who could afford the time and the expense. Dogs were used for coursing in Assyria and ancient Egypt, in much the same way that Greyhounds are still used for coursing rabbits and hares in Ireland today. Dogs were also used for bear baiting and for fighting bulls, other dogs and wild animals. The agricultural land became more open and a great variety of scent hunting dogs were developed for small game in addition to the hounds that were bred for hunting deer, wolves, foxes, hares, otters and badgers.

Selective Breeding

Darwin mentioned three kinds of selection: natural selection, unconscious selection and methodological selection. In the process of natural selection, considerably more offspring are produced than actually reach maturity and substantial variation exists within every population. There is a competition for survival which selects in favor of those individuals best suited to the demands of the immediate environment. Provided that the survivors differ in heredity from those that do not survive, the struggle for existence results in the selection of the fitter genotype. The genotype may be passed on to offspring and after many generations separate strains and races of wolves, jackals, foxes and wild dogs were evolved which were ideally suited for the particular environment. In the process of domestication, the dog was initially modified by unconscious selection, whereby humans preserved the most useful or simply the most esthetically pleasing individuals and allowed these to breed without any special thought of changing the species. Once the potential of the domestic form was realized, there followed a methodological selection for particular characters, in a systematic endeavor to modify the breeds according to some predetermined standard.

Selective breeding is based on the assumption that physical or behavioral characteristics are a reflection of the chromosomal constitution (genes). This is probably true to some extent, but it should be understood that this relationship is not always a perfect correlation and that more usually single genes are not responsible for particular traits. Instead, genetic differences are most probably dictated by a variety of multiple factors rather than simple inheritance.

Problems Associated with Artificial Selection

Despite the many obvious advantages, selective breeding is not without its adverse effects. The rigorous selection and resultant inbreeding for one particular beneficial trait has sometimes produced unfavorable side effects. Moreover, the process of domestication has allowed the survival of individuals that might not have survived in the wild, causing a progressive dilution of the gene pool. Maternal behavior has undergone considerable deterioration mainly because in those cases when the mother does not tend her pups, invariably her offspring are kept alive by bottle feeding. This would tend to perpetuate the genetical framework for that particular behavioral propensity (poor maternal behavior). In other species, maternal behavior has been virtually eliminated, as with domestic hens, in which "broodiness" is viewed as an undesirable trait. In Boston Terrier bitches the pelvis is abnormally narrow and it is often necessary that the pups be delivered by Caesarean section, thus increasing the number of Boston Terriers that are susceptible to this predisposition. In the wild, the bitch would have almost certainly died in labor and the aberrant line would have been discontinued. Similarly, if a valuable stud or

It is imperative not to overlook the importance of temperament when breeding for long sleek coats in Afghan Hounds. The conscientious breeder will be aware of the proper balance, and aim for a dog possessing sound body and mind.

pedigreed bitch refuses to mate, it is becoming more common to use artificial insemination, thus maintaining the strain of poor breeders.

There has been an intense selection for physical characteristics in show dogs, often at the expense of producing adverse changes in temperament. The converse is also true, and inbreeding for desirable behaviors has caused morphological abnormalities in sheepdogs and gun dogs. Certain breeds of dog have an increased susceptibility to disease and several disorders have developed that have a hereditary basis, of which progressive retinal atrophy, Collie eye anomaly and hip dysplasia are probably the best known examples. In some cases, the effects of selective breeding have been more than just an exaggeration of certain desirable traits and instead genetical mutations have intentionally been preserved. The short bowed limbs and out-turned feet of the Dachshund are probably an abnormality which arose from a genetical mutation resulting in chondrodystrophia. This abnormality was deliberately preserved in the Dachshund, presumably because the short strong legs were ideal for the vigorous digging required in badger hunting. Similarly, the long pendulous ears of the Basset Hound were thought to afford protection while hunting badgers and the undershot jaw of the Bulldog enabled it to get a better grip on the bull's nose or lower lip.

Effects of Domestication

Domestication of a relatively few wild species has produced a large number of domestic breeds and strains of dogs, which show considerable variation in behavior and physique. The domestication of dogs led to the establishment of many small breeding populations, probably one in every human settlement in the world. This type of situation was ideally suited for the rapid evolution of particular characters.

Consider, for example, a 200 pound St. Bernard and a ten ounce Yorkshire Terrier, the immense stature of an Irish Wolfhound compared with the diminutive miniature Dachshund; the luxurious coat of a Malamute and the ridiculous five o'clock shadow of a shollo; and the speed of a Greyhound compared with the bumbling bounce of a Bassett Hound. Under the favorable influence of the more clement domestic environment, and with the removal of some of the constraints of natural selection, there is less of a "struggle for survival," and more extreme forms have survived, and in some cases have been selectively bred. It is doubtful that some of the extreme breeds would survive in part of the wild; a Chihuahua in Alaska, a St. Bernard in the Sahara, or a Bassett Hound on the chase would probably meet with little success. Many breeds have lost the adaptability of their wild ancestors, but they are nevertheless superior at those specific functions for which they have been bred, although, in the present day domestic environment, there is often little opportunity for the profitable expression of such talents, as evidenced by the terrier's excavation of the sofa or the Pointer's menacing point at the budgie.

Anatomical Changes. As an overall generalization, it would appear that early types of domesticated animals were smaller than their wild counterparts. In fact, the smaller size is one of the main diagnostic features for distinguishing between wild and domestic remains in prehistoric sites. The introduction of dogs into the

210

household and even into temples and monasteries was probably one of the main selective pressures for breeding smaller dogs, which were much easier to handle, less costly to feed and did not take up as much space. Similarly, there was a reduction in the size of dogs that were used to hunt in packs, which greatly facilitated their husbandry and management. Since that time, there has been a gradual overall miniaturization of breeds (with obvious exceptions). The domestic relaxation of some of the pressures of natural selection has enabled smaller pups, such as the "runt of the litter," to survive. Moreover, in the more sheltered domestic environment, the muscular-skeletal system often remains underdeveloped from lack of exercise and the teeth and jaws fail to develop fully, since domestic dogs are often fed on soft foods. Consequently, there has been a reduction in the size of the chewing muscles and of their bony points of origin and insertion on the skull and lower jaws. These dental changes reflect a decrease in weaponry. A dog's only weapons are its imposing set of teeth and in the wild, "no teeth" would probably be synonymous with "no dog." This selective pressure for survival has been removed by domestication. To keep your dog's teeth in trim, feed it the occasional Nylabone®.

In domestic breeds, the wild coloration seems to be the exception rather than the rule and has only been preserved in a few breeds, such as the German Shepherd Dog, Husky and Malamute. The selective pressure for camouflage has been removed, since humans have alleviated the need for domestic animals to hunt for their food or hide from potential predators. New domestic colorations have evolved: black, white, red, piebald (black and white), skewbald (brown and white) and a mixture of both. The latter colorations are very common in domestic breeds but are rare in nature (e.g., African hunting dog). Such coat patterns are not entirely new, since black, white and red pigments are present in the hair of the wolf and other wild *canidae*. However, by the process of selective breeding, one or more hair pigments have been excluded. In fact, some breeds have little hair at all, such as the Mexican Hairless and the shollo (Xoloitzcuintli), which looks like a spotted Whippet with large, pointed, bat-like ears and a trace of stubble on the dome of its head. It has fewer teeth than other breeds and its body temperature is slightly higher than average. The Mexican Hairless and shollo are thought to be relatives of the

Chinese Crested, an extremely scarce breed with a smooth skin which is covered in blotches of bluish pigmentation. When it reaches maturity, it develops an untidy tuft of wispy white hair on the top of its head.

Loose skin is more usually characteristic of young animals but it has been retained by adults in certain domestic breeds, in which the skin is quite flabby and folds like dewlaps are apparent. This phenomenon is known as *neoteny,* whereby juvenile characteristics are retained in the adult form. In some breeds, there has been an overall shortening of the facial part of the skull compared with the cranium or brain case. This is particularly evident in adult dogs of the mastiff group and has been carried to extremes in breeds such as the Pekingese and Pug.

The shortening of the jaws has in turn produced changes in dentition and on the whole, the teeth of domestic dogs are smaller. In some breeds, the jaw has been reduced to such an extent that there is not sufficient room for the teeth to lie in a single row. In the Bulldog, several teeth overlap and in the Pekingese, the canines are deformed and some of the lower incisors are absent. Bulldogs were bred for baiting bulls and bears, a sport which was popular for several centuries in England until it was made illegal in 1835. The bulldog was supposed to grab the bull by the nose and simply hang on for dear life. The Bulldog also has a receding nose so that it can breath while stuck on the bull's snout. The breed became known for its persistence and tenacity. In actual fact, the Bulldog has an undershot jaw, so that once it has grabbed the bull's snout, the weight of the dog locks the jaw closed and there is no way that the dog could release its hold even if it wanted to. (So much for British doggedness).

Behavioral Changes. A wild animal would normally take flight if approached too closely by a human or other predators. Alternatively, the animal might exhibit a defense reaction if retreat is prevented. The most obvious effects of domestication have been a reduction in the tendency to escape, and an accompanying decrease in aggressiveness. These changes have been brought about largely by the processes of selective breeding and by the provision of food and shelter for those animals growing up in captivity. Similarly, the ability to escape has been further reduced in a number of smaller domestic breeds, which have smaller legs that

The Chinese Crested is a very rare breed with a hairless body. It was originally believed that the Chinese Crested was the result of a mutation, but there is some evidence to suggest that it existed as a pet of the Mandarins in ancient China.

are better equipped for supporting the animal when eating from a dish, rather than covering long distances in the search of food. (In some domestic animals, however, the escape reaction has been preserved, as with thoroughbred horses, in which the "startle" or "flight response" is of considerable advantage in racing).

With the exception of a few aggressive breeds, on the whole, domestic dogs have been selectively bred for docility. This also has been facilitated by smaller body size (and smaller teeth) that allowed for easier management. Moreover, modification of the normal processes of socialization have aided the formation of attachments between dogs and people, which have reduced both the tendency to flee or be aggressive toward humans.

In zoos throughout the world, it has long been realized that it can be extremely difficult to get captive animals to breed successfully. One of the major effects of domestication has been an increase in fertility. This is primarily the result of an extremely strong selective pressure, since obviously only those animals that breed can be selected. In addition, the more favorable domestic environment has certainly had a beneficial effect. In wolves, puberty usually occurs by the end of the second year, whereas domestic dogs may reach maturity as early as the sixth month. Not only do domestic dogs have a longer reproductive life span than wolves, but domestic dogs have two heat periods a year, whereas wolves have only one.

Another factor that has influenced the process of taming is the phenomenon of behavioral *neoteny,* whereby the adult animal tends to retain infantile and juvenile behavior patterns, and wild habits are correspondingly reduced. It is difficult to say exactly how or why these particular traits were bred for. Perhaps the friendliest or the "cutest" dogs were kept and bred, thus unconsciously selecting for those animals that were slow to mature, so that their puppy-like qualities were exaggerated. This is further encouraged during development, especially with many of the toy breeds, which are often treated as perpetual puppies. The puppy-like behavior is forever being reinforced whenever the owner picks up the dog as the bitch might do.

Behavioral neoteny has several adaptive qualities; however, it prevents overspecialization and allows the animal a high degree of behavioral plasticity. (In fact, this behavioral phenomenon has

214

enabled the domestication of the cat, which will often rub against the legs of its owner, or the door of the refrigerator, in much the same way that it would attempt to solicit food as a kitten by rubbing against the legs of its mother).

The domestic selection of breeds for specialized behavioral functions has artificially extended the powers of adaptation within the species. For instance, natural herding tendencies that are utilized by the wolf when hunting caribou have been intensified by selective breeding to produce working breeds for herding sheep and cattle.

The evolution of the modern day gun dogs offers a fine example of how artificial selection has facilitated the exaggeraton of certain behavioral propensities, which were largely dictated by the need for specific hunting characteristics in accordance with improvements in the technology of firearms. In medieval England, birds were hunted with hawks and hounds. Often, bowmen would accompany the hounds in search of stags. General all purpose springer-type spaniels were used to "spring" game into nets, or to retrieve animals that had been killed by the hunters. Cocker Spaniels were similarly used to flush out woodcock. The invention of muzzle-loading "fowling pieces" indicated the need for much slower dogs to enable the hunter to get close enough to the game in order to shoot it on first try, since it would take considerable time to reload. The Pointer was ideally suited for this purpose. It would locate the game, using its well developed senses of smell and hearing, and then remain stationary in the classic Pointer posture, with one foreleg raised and its muzzle "pointing" towards the location of the game. Following a signal from the hunter, the dog would approach with slow and deliberate movements, enabling the huntsman to get a single good shot when the game was flushed. The wolf pauses momentarily before it charges, and this phase has been lengthened by selective breeding in the pointer and setter breeds. The development of breech-loading firearms enables a much quicker working gun dog to be employed. The setters became very popular and would move very quickly to locate the game and then lie down in a "set," indicating the position of the bird, and rapidly flush it out only upon the command of its master. When organized shoots became popular over land that was kept well stocked with game, the rate of kill was considerably greater and all that was needed was a well trained retriever, which would watch where the corpses fell and subsequently collect them up for the hunters.

These traits point to the fact that the behavioral changes of domestication have been *quantitative* rather than *qualitative;* that is, are a matter of degree rather than kind. Various traits of the wolf have been exaggerated by the process of selectively breeding domestic dogs, with the result that there is a much greater variety of anatomical and behavioral types in domestic breeds. However, there appears to be no difference between the basic behavioral repertoires of wolves and dogs, and no behavior has been observed in dogs that has not been seen in their wild counterparts. There is, nevertheless, great variance in the way that wolves and dogs relate to humans. It is the thousands of years of domestication that have made dogs the loyal companions that they are today, whereas wolves remain creatures of the wild.

The Family Pet

When dogs became domesticated and were allowed into human dwellings, they entered into a much closer and special relationship with humans. In the same way that humans are individuals, so are dogs, and similarly each relationship between dog and human is unique. To a large extent, the types of relationships depend on the reasons why the owner has acquired the dog; whether as a necessity (seeing-eye dog), as a working dog (sheepdog, police dog), for recreation (gun dog, show dog), or as a family pet. These considerations largely determine the amount of contact and degree of intimacy between owner and dog.

The family dog is particularly important in the eyes of children. In many ways, the pet may play a significant role in the child's emotional and moral development and education. It is always ready to greet its human companion no matter what the mood of the child. The young owner derives security from the knowledge that he or she is loved. Similarly, the dog represents an object to be loved, which helps to orient the child's attention away from itself. A mutually dependent relationship develops and the child learns that one must love in order to be loved. The pet dog may serve as a useful model for the child, who learns that training and discipline are necessary essentials for acquiring social acceptance.

Equally as important, the child may assume responsibility for looking after the dog and acquire confidence while giving the pet commands. This puts the child at a level on par with adults. Similarly, the pet is a convenient model that may assist explanation of the trickier facts of life, such as sex, birth and death.

Occasionally, relationships between people and their pets assume such a degree of intensity that normal social relationships with other people may be excluded. This type of relationship is perhaps more common between elderly people and their pets. Pets assume a greater importance in the lives of the aged, as their im-

Your family pet, aside from being a loyal companion, can become a sort of model, assisting in the explanation, for your children, of the trickier facts of life, such as the birth of a litter of puppies.

Just as all people have a strong need to love and be loved, so does a dog. If a pet is lacking in the necessary affection he needs to thrive on, he may take to periods of restlessness, and begin to develop self-destructive tendencies out of boredom and frustration.

mediate circle of friends becomes smaller. Sometimes there is a corresponding decline in status; the elderly are forced to retire, or are sent to special homes, and gradually they are alienated from society. Like all people, they have the need to love and be loved, and to communicate with their friends. However, it is often the case that very few people are interested in taking the time or patience to talk to elderly people or listen to their reminiscences. In some cases, a dog may be the person's only living friend, fulfilling the need of having someone to love, allowing the owner to feel wanted and needed. For some people who grow old, life loses much of its meaning, since they feel that it is much too late in life to start a new venture. Keeping a pet is an ideal hobby. The dog is a useful topic of conversation when meeting people, and of course, the need to walk the dog also ensures that its owner is adequately exercised.

This section has been mainly concerned with the very young dog owners and the elderly. However, at this point it might be worthwhile to bear in mind a few choice words from Robert Benchley: "There is no doubt that every healthy, normal boy (if there is such a thing in these days of Child Study) should own a dog at some time in his life, preferably between the ages of 45 and 50." The family dog offers a source of unconditional acceptance and affection towards its owners. All it needs in return is a little human friendship and understanding. In most households the dog soon becomes a symbol of faithfulness and good companionship; more often than not, a symbol that invariably occupies the most comfortable armchair in the home.

Index